John Zundel

Christian Heart Songs

John Zundel

Christian Heart Songs

ISBN/EAN: 9783337334611

Printed in Europe, USA, Canada, Australia, Japan

Cover: Foto ©Thomas Meinert / pixelio.de

More available books at **www.hansebooks.com**

CHRISTIAN HEART-SONGS:

A COLLECTION OF

Solos, Quartetts, and Choruses,

OF ALL METERS,

TOGETHER WITH

A SELECTION OF CHANTS AND SET PIECES.

BY

JOHN ZUNDEL,

AUTHOR OF "MODERN SCHOOL FOR THE ORGAN," "TREATISE ON HARMONY AND MODULATION," AND VARIOUS WORKS FOR THE CHOIR, ORGAN, AND MELODEON.

NEW YORK:

J. B. FORD AND COMPANY.

ZUNDEL AND BRAND, TOLEDO, OHIO,

AGENTS FOR THE MUSIC TRADE.

1870.

PREFACE.

THE peculiar form and limited extent of this work prove that it is not offered in competition with the large and new collections appearing every season. I shall be content to see my labors appreciated by that rapidly increasing number of individuals, choirs, teachers of sacred music, and musical associations, who desire to obtain genuine new music of a higher order than common, yet eminently fitted for religious worship and for practice. The music offered here is not difficult to read; the greater difficulty consists in understanding and rendering its spirit. Well-educated leaders, such as love song not merely for salary's sake, will welcome, I trust, the advent of this work. If length of time in preparation be taken as any evidence of excellence, "Christian Heart-Songs" may claim some share of worth, for it has required almost a lifetime to compose its contents. The tunes are either the outpourings of a full heart, or were composed to meet keenly felt wants for music suited to certain poetry or to special occasions; and the larger proportion have been sung and criticised before their insertion in this book. A limited number of the pieces here presented were many years ago printed under the title of "The Choral Friend," and were warmly welcomed by the few musical people whom the small edition could reach, and honored with very flattering notices of the press.

Influenced by the differences of mode and spirit in which music was conducted in the churches where I have been engaged during the last twenty-four years, the tunes will be found to be of a greater variety than might be expected from one and the same authorship. During my short stay in the First Unitarian Church in Brooklyn, and St. George's (Dr. Tyng's) in New York, I composed mainly tunes for quartette singing (Ropes, Bainbridge, Clara, Lafon, Morning, Sampson, etc.), and some Episcopal music;* but by far the greater portion, composed during my now nearly eighteen years' connection with Plymouth (Rev. H. W. Beecher's) Church, have been written with a view to their use by large choirs, or perhaps in congregational singing.

The frequent pretence of the adversaries of congregational singing, that the American people are not sufficiently musically educated for its introduction, is quite absurd. As a German-born citizen, I may take the liberty of saying that, superior as musical education in Germany may be, or even is, church singing has little profited by it. The Germans sing their chorals mostly after hearing them,

---

* A number of pages furnish also tunes composed with the special view of serving for choir practice and for the singing-class. These are Hosanna, Ansonia, Crystal, Lexington, Fischer, Indianapolis, Trenton, Providence, etc.

—they learn them partly at school, and the parents sing them to the children from generation to generation. To introduce a new choral into a congregation is no less trouble than to make a new tune go in any American church, provided the tune be singable and enjoyable at all. Now, let churches wishing for congregational singing get a good, substantial (not all over sweet and only sweet) *organ*, with good diapasons and better bass, and as few brass and mixture stops as possible; find a good *organist* and leader, — one who is a Christian man, one who *sincerely* loves congregational singing; gather a good, large, well-balanced *choir* of not less than twelve good voices for a church holding not only, but *having*, an audience of from eight hundred to a thousand people. Let this choir sing their anthems as sweetly as they can; yet do not permit them to sing every Sunday to every hymn a new tune, but cause them to repeat a certain tune say two or three Sundays in succession, and notice whether the tune gains in favor with choir *and* congregation. If the new tune takes well, keep it; repeat it in the lecture-room, in the prayer-meeting, at home; and thus go on until you have found and learned to sing all the tunes needed. Congregational singing cannot be introduced into churches by vote or decree, still less by the introduction of a bulky tune-book. Congregational tune-books should not contain more than one half the tunes they are stuffed with at present, their great bulk making them expensive, and thereby preventing the introduction of new books with improved music and hymns, — for American congregations are not likely to stand still, but will keep pace in their musical worship with the progress made outside the church.

A few words now about the present work. The figures under the head of "Time," in the Index, give the number of seconds required for the singing of one verse of the tune or hymn. Varying size, or different acoustic proportions of churches, more or less crowded houses, etc., may require more or less modification. Under peculiar circumstances a change of the key of the tunes may be justified. It was found necessary, for example, during our last war, to play many tunes even a whole tone higher than they were written.

All the music contained in the work being composed or harmonized by the author, or written by others for this work (pp. 69, 114, 143), and covered by copyright, parties wishing to copy will be accommodated on application to either author or publishers.

In conclusion, I would say that I hope this work, even as far only as mere mechanical or artistic improvement is concerned, will do some good. But unless the tunes are rightly interpreted, unless they are sung in the spirit that conceived them, the best purpose of the work — true musical worship, impressive edification — will be lost. How shall this spirit be obtained? Just in the same way that we try to obtain other graces. Watch and pray for it; get Christian organists and leaders; put no profane people, good singers as they may be, into your choirs; and then why not pray for your church music while you are praying for your pastors, deacons, Sunday schools, etc.? I hold that choirs are worth praying for: I know they need praying for: and I trust none will say they are past praying for.

                                                            JOHN ZUNDEL.

BROOKLYN, N. Y., September, 1870.

CHRISTIAN HEART-SONGS.

HOSANNA. L. M.

Z.

Tenor.

1. Now to the Lord a no - ble song! A - wake, my soul! a - wake, my tongue! Ho -
2. See where it shines in Je - sus' face, The bright-est im - age of his grace; God,

Treble.

Alto.

Bass.

san - na to th' e - ter - nal name, And all his bound - less love pro - claim.
in the per - son of his Son, Has all his migh - tiest works out - done.

3 The spacious earth and spreading flood,
Proclaim the wise and powerful God;
And thy rich glories from afar
Sparkle in every rolling star.

4 But in his looks a glory stands,
The noblest labor of thine hands:
The pleasing lustre of his eyes
Outshines the wonders of the skies.

5 Grace! 'tis a sweet, a charming theme;
My thoughts rejoice at Jesus' name;
Ye angels, dwell upon the sound!
Ye heavens, reflect it to the ground!

6 O may I live to reach the place
Where he unveils his lovely face!
Where all his beauties you behold.
And sing his name to harps of gold!

ROPES. L. M.

Z.

O hap-py day, that fixed my choice On thee, my Sa - vior, and my Lord! Well

may this glow-ing heart re-joice, And tell its rap - ture all a-broad.

BENEFACTOR. L. M.

Z.

A - way from eve-ry mor - tal care, A - way from earth, our souls retreat; We

leave this worth - less world a - far, And wait and wor - ship near thy seat.

Z.

1. An - o-ther six day's work is done; An - o - ther Sab - bath is be - gun; Re -

turn, my soul, en - joy thy rest, Im - prove the day thy God hath

blessed, Improve the day thy God hath blessed.

m. v.

m. v

2 O that our thoughts and thanks may rise,
As grateful incense to the skies;
And draw from heaven that sweet repose
Which none but he that feels it knows!

3 This heavenly calm within the breast
Is the dear pledge of glorious rest,
Which for the church of God remains ;—
The end of cares, the end of pains.

4 In holy duties let the day,
In holy pleasures pass away;
How sweet a Sabbath thus to spend,
In hope of one that ne'er shall end !

Ropes.

2 O happy bond, that seals my vows
  To him who merits all my love !
Let cheerful anthems fill his house,
  While to that sacred shrine I move.

3 'T is done—the great transaction's done :
  I am the Lord's, and he is mine ;
He drew me, and I followed on,
  Charmed to confess the voice divine.

4 High heaven, that heard the solemn vow,
  That vow renewed shall daily hear
Till in life's latest hour I bow,
  And bless, in death, a bond so dear.

Benefactor.

1 Away from every mortal care,
  Away from earth, our souls retreat;
We leave this worthless world afar,
  And wait and worship near thy seat.

2 Lord ! in the temple of thy grace,
  We see thy feet and we adore;
We gaze upon thy lovely face,
  And learn the wonders of thy power.

3 Father ! my soul would still abide
  Within thy temple, near thy side;
But if my feet must hence depart,
  Still keep thy dwelling in my heart.

THE STAR OF BETHLEHEM. L. M. (Double.)

Z.

1. When marshaled on the night-ly plain, The glittering host be - stud the sky, One

mf

Organ bass.

star a - lone, of all the train, Can fix the sin - ner's wandering eye.

Hark! hark! to God the cho - rus breaks, From eve - ry host, from eve - ry gem;

But

Organ.

But one alone the Sa - vior speaks; It is the Star of Beth - le - hem.

one a - lone, the

f

But one a-lone tho

1. E - ter - nal Source of eve-ry joy! Well may thy praise our lips em-ploy, While

in thy tem - ple we ap-pear, Whose good-ness crowns the cir-cling year.

Star of Bethlehem.

2 Once on the raging seas I rode,
  The storm was loud, the night was dark ;
The ocean yawn'd and rudely blow'd
  The wind that toss'd my found'ring bark.

Deep horror then my vitals froze !
  Death-struck,—I ceased the tide to stem ;
When suddenly a star arose—
  It was the Star of Bethlehem !

It was my guide, my light, my all:
  It bade my dark forebodings cease :
And through the storm and danger's thrall,
  It led me to the port of peace.

Now safely moor'd, my perils o'er,
  Nor raging waves my bark condemn,
Forever, and forevermore,
  I'll sing the Star of Bethlehem.

Missouri.

1 Eternal Source of every joy !
  Well may thy praise our lips employ,
While in thy temple we appear,
  Whose goodness crowns the circling year.

2 Wide as the wheels of nature roll,
  Thy hand supports and guides the whole !
The sun is taught by thee to rise,
  And darkness when to veil the skies.

3 The flowery spring, at thy command,
  Perfumes the air and paints the land ;
The summer rays with vigor shine
  To raise the corn and cheer the vine.

4 Thy hand in autumn richly pours
  Through all our coast redundant stores ;
And winters, softened by thy care,
  No more the face of horror wear.

5 Seasons, and months, and weeks, and days,
  Demand successive songs of praise ;
And be the grateful homage paid
  With morning light and evening shade.

6 Here in thy house let incense rise,
  And circling Sabbaths bless our eyes,
Till to those lofty hights we soar,
  Where days and years revolve no more.

VICTOR. L. M.

Z.

1. How blest the sa - cred tie that binds, In u - nion sweet, ac - cord-ing minds! How

swift the heavenly course they run, Whose hearts, and faith, and hopes are one!

NEWTOWN. L. M.

Z.

1. King-doms and thrones to God be - long; Crown him, ye na-tions, in your song; His

won-drous names and powers re-hearse; His ho - nors shall en - rich your verse.

ST. PETERSBURGH, L. M. 6 lines.

Russian Evening Hymn.—BORTNIANSKY.

1. When gath - 'ring storms a - round I view, And days are dark, and
On him I lean who, not in vain, Ex - pe - rienced eve - ry

1st time. 2nd time.

friends are few; } He sees my wants, al - lays my fears, And
Omit. . . . . hu - man pain. }

counts and trea - sures up my tears.

2 If aught should tempt my soul to stray
From heavenly wisdom's narrow way,
To fly the good I would pursue,
Or do the ill I would not do:
Still he who felt temptation's power
Will guard me in that dangerous hour.

3 When, mourning, o'er some stone I bend,
Which covers all that was a friend:
And from his hand, his voice, his smile,
Divides me for a little while—
My Savior marks the tears I shed,
For "Jesus wept" o'er Lazarus dead.

4 And Oh! when I have safely passed
Through every conflict, but the last,
Still, Lord, unchanging, watch beside
My dying bed, for thou hast died:
Then point to realms of cloudless day,
And wipe the latest tear away.

Vietor.

2 To each, the soul of each how dear!
What jealous love, what holy fear!
How doth the generous flame within
Refine from earth, and cleanse from sin!

3 Their streaming eyes together flow,
For human guilt and mortal woe;
Their ardent prayers together rise,
Like mingling flames in sacrifice.

4 Together oft they seek the place
Where God reveals his awful face;
And they shall meet in realms above,
A heaven of joy—because of love.

Newtown.

1 Kingdoms and thrones to God belong;
Crown him, ye nations, in your song;
His wondrous names and powers rehearse;
His honors shall enrich your verse.

2 He shakes the heavens with loud alarms;
How terrible is God in arms!
In Israel are his mercies known,
Israel is his peculiar throne.

3 Proclaim him King, pronounce him blest;
He's your defence, your joy, your rest;
When terrors rise, and nations faint,
God is the strength of every saint.

ORION. L. M. Double.

Z.

The heavens de - clare thy glo - ry, Lord! In eve - ry star thy wisdom

shines; But when our eyes be - hold thy word, We read thy name in fair - er

lines; The roll-ing sun, the changing light, And nights and days thy power con -

fess; But the blest vol - ume thou hast writ, Reveals thy jus - tice and thy grace.

Choral.

Author unknown, from the 16th Century.

1. "Come hith-er, all ye wea-ry souls! Ye hea-vy-la-den sin-ners! come: I'll

give you rest from all your toils, And raise you to my heavenly home, And

raise you to my heaven-ly home.

2 " They shall find rest who learn of me —
I'm of a meek and lowly mind;
But passion rages like the sea,
And pride is restless as the wind.

3 " Blest is the man whose shoulders take
My yoke, and bear it with delight:
My yoke is easy to his neck,
My grace shall make the burden light."

4 Jesus ! we come at thy command;
With faith, and hope, and humble zeal,
Resign our spirits to thy hand,
To mould and guide us at thy will.

Orion.

1 The heavens declare thy glory, Lord !—
In every star thy wisdom shines;
But when our eyes behold thy word,
We read thy name in fairer lines.

2 The rolling sun, the changing light,
And nights and days thy power confess ·
But the blest volume thou hast writ,
Reveals thy justice and thy grace.

3 Sun, moon, and stars convey thy praise
Round the whole earth, and never stand;
So when thy truth began its race,
It touched and glanced on every land.

Orion (continued.)

4 Nor shall thy spreading gospel rest,
Till through the world thy truth has run,
Till Christ has all the nations blest,
That see the light or feel the sun.

5 Great Sun of Righteousness ! arise,
Bless the dark world with heavenly light;
Thy gospel makes the simple wise ;
Thy laws are pure, thy judgments right.

6 Thy noblest wonders here we view,
In souls renewed and sins forgiven:
Lord ! cleanse my sins, my soul renew,
And make thy word my guide to heaven.

HERMAN. L. M.

German Choral. Herman Schein, anno 1628.

DAYBREAK. L. M.

Z.

1. Great Shep-herd of thine Is - ra - el, Who did'st be-tween the che - rubs dwell, And

lead the tribes, thy cho - sen sheep, Safe through the de - sert and the deep:—Safe

through the de - sert and the deep:—

2 Thy church is in the desert now;
Shine from on high and guide us through
Turn us to thee, thy love restore,—
We shall be saved and sigh no more.

3 Great God, whom heavenly hosts obey,
How long shall we lament and pray,
And wait in vain thy kind return?
How long shall thy fierce anger burn?

4 Instead of wine and cheerful bread,
Thy saints with their own tears are fed;
Turn us to thee, thy love restore,—
We shall be saved and sigh no more.

Herman.

2 My flesh would rest in thine abode,
My panting heart cries out for God;
My God! my King! why should I be
So far from all my joys and thee?

3 Blest are the saints who sit on high,
Around thy throne of majesty;
Thy brightest glories shine above,
And all their work is praise and love.

4 Blest are the souls who find a place
Within the temple of thy grace;
There they behold thy gentler rays,
And seek thy face and learn thy praise.

5 Cheerful they walk, with growing strength,
Till all shall meet in heaven at length—
Till all before thy face appear,
And join in nobler worship there.

Daybreak.

1 O God thou art my God alone;
Early to thee my soul shall cry,—
A pilgrim in a land unknown,
A thirsty land whose springs are dry.

2 Yet through this rough and thorny maze,
I follow hard on thee, my God;
Thy hand unseen upholds my ways,
I safely tread where thou hast trod.

3 Thee, in the watches of the night,
When I remember on my bed,
Thy presence makes the darkness light;
Thy guardian wings are round my head

4 Better than life itself thy love,
Dearer than all beside to me;
For whom have I in heaven above,
Or what on earth compared with thee

BETHLEHEM. L. M. (Double.)

Z.

When marshalled on the nightly plain, The glittering host be-stud the sky, One star a-

lone, of all the train, Can fix the sinner's wandering eye. Hark! hark! to God the chorus

breaks From every host, from every gem; But one a-lone the Savior speaks,—It is the

Star of Bethle-hem; But one a-lone the Savior speaks,—It is the Star of Beth-le-hem.

CHORAL.

1. Great God, at-tend, while Zi-on sings The joy that from thy presence springs; To

spend one day with thee on earth, Ex-ceeds a thou-sand days of mirth.

Beth'lehem.

2 Once on the raging seas I rode,
  The storm was loud, the night was dark,—
The ocean yawned—and rudely blowed
  The wind that tossed my foundering bark.
Deep horror then my vitals froze,
  Death-struck, I ceased the tide to stem;—
When suddenly a star arose,—
  It was the Star of Bethlehem.

3 It was my guide, my light, my all;
  It bade my dark forebodings cease;
And through the storm, and danger's thrall,
  It led me to the port of peace.
Now safely moored—my perils o'er,
  I'll sing, first in night's diadem,
Forever and for evermore,
  The Star—the Star of Bethlehem!

Ararat.

2 Might I enjoy the meanest place
  Within thy house, O God of grace,
Not tents of ease, nor thrones of power,
  Should tempt my feet to leave thy door.

3 God is our sun—he makes our day;
  God is our shield—he guards our way
From all th' assaults of hell and sin,
  From foes without and foes within.

4 All needful grace will God bestow,
  And crown that grace with glory too;
He gives us all things, and withholds
  No real good from upright souls.

5 O God our King, thy sovereign sway
  The glorious hosts of heaven obey,
And devils at thy presence flee;
  Blest is the man that trusts in thee!

2

CLARA. L. M.

Sweet peace of conscience, heavenly guest, | Come, fix thy mansion in my breast ; | Dis-

- pel my doubts, my fears control, | And heal the anguish of my soul.

BLADENBURGII. L. M.

My Shepherd is the liv - ing Lord : | Now shall my wants be well sup-plied: |

IIis providence and ho - ly word | Be-come my safe - ty and my guide.

1. My suff'rings all to Thee are known, Tempted in ev - ery point like me;
2. For whom didst thou the cross en-dure? Who nailed thy bo - dy to the tree?

Re-gard my grief, re - gard Thine own: Je-sus, re - mem-ber Cal - va - ry!
Did not Thy death my life pro-cure? O let Thy mer - cy an-swer me.

3 Art Thou not touched with human woe?
  Hath pity left the Son of man?
Dost Thou not all my sorrow know,
  And claim a share in all my pain?

4 Thou wilt not break a bruised reed,
  Or quench the smallest spark of grace,
Till through the soul thy power is spread,
  Thy all-victorious righteousness.

5 The day of small and feeble things,
  I know Thou never wilt despise;
I know, with healing in His wings,
  The Sun of righteousness shall rise.

Bladenburg.

1 My shepherd is the living Lord;
  Now shall my wants be well supplied;
His providence and holy word
  Become my safety and my guide.

2 In pastures where salvation grows,
  He makes me feed, he makes me rest;
There living water gently flows,
  And all the food's divinely blest.

3 My wandering feet his ways mistake;
  But he restores my soul to peace,
And leads me, for his mercy's sake,
  In the fair paths of righteousness.

4 Though I walk through the gloomy vale
  Where death and all its terrors are,
My heart and hope shall never fail,
  For God my shepherd's with me there.

Clara.

1 How sweet to leave the world awhile,
  And seek the presence of our Lord!
Dear Saviour! on thy people smile,
  And come, according to thy word.

2 From busy scenes we now retreat,
  That we may here converse with Thee;
Ah! Lord! behold us at Thy feet;
  Let this the "gate of heaven" be.

3 "Chief of ten thousand!" now appear,
  That we by faith may see Thy face:
Oh! speak, that we Thy voice may hear,
  And let Thy presence fill this place.

Jesus shall reign where'er the sun | Does his suc-cessive journeys run; | His

kingdom stretch from shore to shore, | Till moons shall wax and wane no more.

SARAH. L. M. z.

pp or Soli. *ff*

f 'Tis by the faith of joys to come | We walk thro' deserts dark as night; | Till

pp or Soli. *mf*

we arrive at heaven, our home, | Faith is our guide, and faith our light.

1. How blest the right-eous when he dies! How sinks a wea-ry soul to rest! How

2. So fades a sum-mer cloud a-way; So sinks the gale when storms are o'er; So

mild-ly beam the clos-ing eyes! How gent-ly heaves th'ex-pir-ing breast!

gent-ly shuts the eye of day; So dies the wave a-long the shore.

3 A holy quiet reigns around,
   A calm which life nor death destroys;
And naught disturbs that peace profound
   Which his unfettered soul enjoys.

4 Farewell, conflicting hopes and fears,
   Where lights and shades alternate dwell;
How bright th'unchanging morn appears!
   Farewell, inconstant world, farewell!

5 Life's labor done, as sinks the clay,
   Light from the load the spirit flies,
While heaven and earth combine to say,
   "How blest the righteous when he dies!"

Ingraham.

2 For Him shall endless prayer be made,
   And praises throng to crown His head;
His name, like sweet perfume, shall rise
   With every morning sacrifice.

3 People and realms of every tongue
   Dwell on His love with sweetest song;
And infant voices shall proclaim
   Their early blessings on His name.

4 Blessings abound where'er He reigns;
   The prisoner leaps to lose his chains;
The weary find eternal rest,
   And all the sons of want are blest.

5 Let every creature rise and bring
   Peculiar honors to their King:
Angels descend with songs again,
   And earth repeat the long amen.

Sarah.

2 The want of light she well supplies,
   She makes the pearly gates appear;
Far into distant worlds she pries,
   And brings eternal glories near.

3 Cheerful we tread the desert through,
   While faith inspires a heavenly ray,
Though lions roar, and tempests blow,
   And rocks and dangers fill the way.

4 So Abr'am, by divine command,
   Left his own house to walk with God;
His faith beheld the promised land,
   And fired his zeal along the road.

1. Great God, our strength, to thee we cry, Oh let us not for-got-ten lie; Op-

pressed with sor-rows and with care, To thy pro-tec-tion we re-pair. O

let thy light at-tend our way, Thy truth af-ford its stea-dy ray; To

Zi-on's hill di-rect our feet, To wor-ship at thy sa-cred seat.

* Tenor and Base—or all parts.

1. My God, ac-cept my ear-ly vows, Like morn-ing in-cense in thy house; And

let my night-ly wor-ship rise, Sweet as the eve-ning sa-cri-fice.

Supplication.

1 Great God, our strength, to thee we cry,
O let us not forgotten lie:
Oppressed with sorrows and with care,
To thy protection we repair.

2 O let thy light attend our way,
Thy truth afford its steady ray;
To Zion's hill direct our feet,
To worship at thy sacred seat.

3 Thy praise, O God, shall tune the lyre,
Thy love our joyful song inspire;
To thee our cordial thanks be paid,
Our sure defence, our constant aid.

4 Why, then, cast down, and why distressed?
And whence the grief, that fills our breast?
In God we'll hope, to God we'll raise
Our songs of gratitude and praise.

Watts.

1 My God! accept my early vows,
Like morning-incense in thy house;
And let my nightly worship rise,
Sweet as the evening sacrifice.

2 Watch o'er my lips, and guard them, Lord!
From every rash and heedless word;
Nor let my feet incline to tread
The guilty path where sinners lead.

3 Oh! may the righteous, when I stray,
Smite, and reprove my wandering way;
Their gentle words, like ointment shed,
Shall never bruise, but cheer my head.

4 When I behold them pressed with grief,
I'll cry to heaven for their relief;
And, by my warm petitions prove
How much I prize their faithful love

PACIFIC. L. M. (DOUBLE.)

ARRANGED.

My God, per-mit me not to be | A stranger to myself and thee : | A -

- midst a thou-sand thoughts I rove, | For-get-ful of my highest love. | Why

should my pas-sions mix with earth, | And thus de-base my heavenly birth ? | Why

should I cleave to things be - low, | And let my God, my Sa - viour, go ?

1. O Christ, be - fore whose cross we fall, Who bend - est to the
2. O Thou, by whom the lost are found, Thy cross, un - seen, on

bend - ed knee, Who spurn - est none, who lov - est all, To
Cal - v'ry stands,—Whose ho - ly sha - dow on the ground Creeps

Thee, from ev - ery land and sea, Thy fa - ther's err - ing
east and west through ma - ny lands Un - til it wraps the

chil - dren call! Thy fa - ther's err - ing chil - dren call!
world a - round! Un - til it wraps the world a - round!

3 O Thou who conquerest by this sign,
  Who taketh praise from human speech,—
To every zone, from palm to pine,
  Each human heart is bound to each,
    And by Thy cross is bound to thine!

4 O Thou who clearest men from sin,
  For whom the whole earth, groaning, waits,
Make Thou all men by love akin,
  And through the everlasting gates
    Lead all Thy father's children in!

THEO. TILTON.

PARADISE. L. M. Double.

Arr. by J. Z.

1. When Jor-dan hush'd his wa-ters still, And si-lence slept on Zi-on's hill,
2. On wheels of light, on wings of flame, The glorious hosts of Zi-on came;

When Bethlehem's shepherds thro' the night, Watch'd o'er their flocks by starry light,—
High heaven with songs of triumph rung, While thus they struck their harps and sung:

Hark! from the midnight hills a-round, A voice of more than mor-tal sound,
"O Zi-on, lift thy raptured eye; The long-ex-pect-ed hour is nigh;

In dis-tant hal-le-lu-jahs stole,

In dis-tant hal-le-lu-jahs stole, Wild murmuring o'er the raptured soul.
The joys of na-ture rise a-gain; The Prince of Sa-lem comes to reign.

3 "See, Mercy, from her golden urn,
Pours a rich stream to them that mourn;
Behold, she binds, with tender care,
The bleeding bosom of despair.
He comes to cheer the tender heart;
Bids Satan and his host depart;
Again the day-star gilds the gloom,
Again the bowers of Eden bloom."

1. When marshalled on the night-ly plain, The glittering host be-stud the sky,

One star a - lone, of all the train, Can fix the sin - ner's wandering eye.

Pacific.

2 Call me away from flesh and sense;
   One sovereign word can draw me thence;
   I would obey the voice divine,
   And all inferior joys resign.

3 Be earth, with all her scenes withdrawn;
   Let noise and vanity be gone:
   In secret silence of the mind
   My heaven, and there my God, I find.

———

* The singing of the unison passage without accompaniment, and adding a powerful Organ to the chords marked × × will produce an excellent effect.

Lincoln

2 Hark! hark! to God the chorus breaks,
   From every host, from every gem;
   But one alone the Saviour speaks—
   It is the Star of Bethlehem.

3 Once on the raging seas I rode,
   The storm was loud, the night was dark;
   The ocean yawned, and rudely blowed
   The wind that tossed my foundering bark.

4 Deep horror then my vitals froze,
   Death-struck, I ceased the tide to stem;
   When suddenly a Star arose—
   It was the Star of Bethlehem.

5 It was my guide, my light, my all;
   It bade my dark foreboding cease;
   And through the storm, and danger's thrall,
   It led me to the port of peace.

6 Now safely moored—my perils o'er
   I'll sing, first in night's diadem,
   For ever and for evermore,
   The Star—the Star of Bethlehem!

NEANDER. L. M. 6 lines.

Arranged.

1. The Lord my pas-ture shall prepare, And feed me with a shepherd's care; His

pres-ence shall my wants sup - ply, And guard me with a watch-ful eye; My

noon - day walks he will at - tend, And all my mid - night hours defend

1 The Lord my pasture shall prepare,
And feed me with a shepherd's care;
His presence shall my wants supply,
— And guard me with a watchful eye;
My noon-day walks he will attend,
And all my midnight hours defend.

2 When in the sultry glebe I faint,
Or on the thirsty mountain pant,
To fertile vales and dewy meads
My weary, wandering steps he leads,
Where peaceful rivers, soft and slow,
Amid the verdant landscape flow

3 Though in a bare and rugged way,
Through devious, lonely wilds I stray,
Thy presence shall my pains beguile;
The barren wilderness shall smile,
With sudden greens and herbage crowned,
And streams shall murmur all around.

4 Though in the paths of death I tread,
With gloomy horrors overspread,
My steadfast heart shall know no ill,
For thou, O Lord! art with me still;
Thy friendly rod shall give me aid,
And guide me through the dreadful shade

Join, all ye ser-vants of the Lord, | To praise him for his sacred word, | That

word, like manna, sent from heaven, | To all who seek, is free-ly given: | Its

prom-i-ses our fears re-move, | And fill our hearts with joy and love.

2.
It tells us, though oppressed with cares,
The God of mercy hears our prayers;
Though steep and rough the appointed way,
His mighty arm shall be our stay;
Though deadly foes assail our peace,
His power shall bid their malice cease.

3.
It tells who first inspired our breath,
And who redeemed our souls from death:
It tells of grace, grace freely given,
And shows the path to God and heaven:
O bless we then our gracious Lord,
For all the treasures of his word!

ROSE. C. M.

One prayer I have, all prayers in one, | When I am wholly thine;

Thy will, my God, thy will be done, | And let that will be mine.

TRENTON. C. M.

Bold.

Come, shout a - loud the Fa - ther's grace, | And sing the Saviour's love ; | Soon

shall you join the glo - rious theme, | In lof - tier strains a - bove.

1. La - den with guilt, and full of fears, I fly to Thee, my Lord;

And not a ray of hope ap - pears, But in Thy writ - ten word.

Rose.

2 All-wise, almighty, and all-good,
　　In Thee I firmly trust ;
Thy ways, unknown or understood.
　　Are merciful and just.

3 May I remember that to thee
　　Whate'er I have I owe ;
And back, in gratitude, from me
　　May all thy bounty flow.

8 And though thy wisdom takes away,
　　Shall I arraign thy will ?
No, let me bless thy name, and say,
　　" The Lord is gracious still."

4 A pilgrim through the earth I roam,
　　Of nothing long possessed,
And all must fail when I go home,
　　For this is not my home.

_____

Trenton.

2 God, the eternal, mighty God,
　　To dearer names descends ;
Calls you his treasure and his joy
　　His children and his friends.

3 My Father, God! and may these lips
　　Pronounce a name so dear ?
Not thus could heaven's sweet harmony
　　Delight my listening ear.

4 Thanks to my God for every gift
　　His bounteous hands bestow ;
And thanks eternal for that love
　　Whence all those comforts flow.

_____

Vasar.

2 The volume of my Father's grace
　　Does all my grief assuage ;
Here I behold my Saviour's face
　　In almost every page.

3 This is the field where hidden lies
　　The pearl of price unknown ;
That merchant is divinely wise
　　Who makes the pearl his own.

4 This is the judge that ends the strife
　　Where wit and reason fail ;
My guide to everlasting life
　　Through all this gloomy vale.

Allegretto.

1. In thee I put my steadfast trust, | De-fend me, Lord, from shame; | In
3. My steadfast and unchanging hope | Shall on thy power depend; | And

Fine.

. . cline thine ear, and save my soul, | For righteous is . . . thy name.
I, in grateful songs of praise, | My time to come . . will spend.

SOLO. Treble, or Tenor.

2. Be thou my strong a - bid - ing place, | To which I may resort; | Thy

Accomp.

D. C.

promise, Lord, is my defence, | Thou art my rock and fort.

D. C.

1. My God, my por-tion and my love, My ev-er-last-ing all, I've

I've none but thee in heav'n above, Or on this earth-ly ball.

none but thee in heav'n a-bove, Or on this earth - - ly ball.

Instr.

Bainbridge.

1 My God, my portion, and my love,
My everlasting all ;
I've none but thee in heaven above,
Or on this earthly ball.

2 To thee we owe our wealth and friends,
And health, and safe abode ;
Thanks to thy name for meaner things,
But they are not my God.

3 How vain a toy is glittering wealth,
If once compared to thee !
Or what's my safety, or my health,
Or all my friends to me !

4 If I possessed the spacious earth,
And called the stars my own ;
Without thy graces and thyself,
I were a wretch undone.

5 Let others stretch their arms like seas,
And grasp in all the shore ;
Grant me the visits of thy face,
And I desire no more.

Bainbridge.

1 Jerusalem ! my happy home !
Name ever dear to me !
When shall my labors have an end
In joy, and peace, and thee ?

2 When shall these eyes thy heaven-built walls
And pearly gates behold ?
Thy bulwarks with salvation strong,
And streets of shining gold ?

3 There happier bowers than Eden's bloom
Nor sin nor sorrow know :
Blessed seats ! thro' rude and stormy scenes
I onward press to you.

4 Why should I shrink at pain and woe ?
Or feel at death dismay ?
I've Canaan's goodly land in view,
And realms of endless day.

4 Apostles, martyrs, prophets, there
Around my Saviour stand ;
And soon my friends in Christ below
Will join the heavenly band.

6 Jerusalem ! my happy home !
My soul still pants for thee ;
Then shall my labors have an end
When I thy joys shall see.

Z.

1. Lord, thou wilt hear me when I pray; I am for-e-ver thine: I

fear be-fore thee all the day, Nor would I dare to sin. And

while I rest my wea-ry head, From cares and bus' - ness free; 'T is

sweet con-vers - ing on my bed, With my own heart and thee.

1. With cheer - ful notes let all the earth To heaven their
2. God's ten - der mer - cy knows no bound, His truth shall

voic - - - es raise; Let all, in - spired with
ne'er de - cay; Then let the will - ing

god - ly mirth, Sing sol - emn hymns of praise.
na - tions round, Their grate - ful trib - ute pay.

Evening Devotion.

1 Lord! thou wilt hear me when I pray,
　I am for ever thine;
　I fear before thee all the day,
　Nor would I dare to sin.

2 And while I rest my weary head,
　From cares and business free,
　'Tis sweet conversing on my bed
　With my own heart and thee.

3 I pay this evening sacrifice;
　And when my work is done,
　Great God! my faith, my hope relies
　Upon thy grace alone.

4 Thus, with my thoughts composed to peace
　I'll give mine eyes to sleep;
　Thy hand in safety keeps my days,
　And will my slumbers keep.

When storms hang o'er the Christian's head, | He flies un - to his God, | And under his re - fresh-ing shade, | Finds a secure a - bode, | When foes without, and fears within, | Seek to dis-turb his peace, | To God he makes his sorrows known, And straight his sorrows cease.

And under his re - fresh-ing shade

To God he makes his sorrows known,

How bless'd are they who al-ways keep | The pure and per-fect way;

Who nev-er from the sa-cred paths | Of God's commandments stray!

NOTE. The last measure but one can be omitted.

Sampson.

1 Sweet day! so cool, so calm, so bright,
  Bridal of earth and sky;
The dew shall weep thy fall to-night,
  For thou, alas! must die.

2 Sweet rose! in air whose odors wave,
  And colors charm the eye;
Thy root is ever in the grave,
  And thou, alas! must die.

3 Sweet spring! of days and roses made,
  Whose charms for beauty vie,
Thy days depart, thy roses fade,
  Thou, too, alas! must die.

4 Only a sweet and holy soul
  Hath tints that never fly;
While flowers decay, and seasons roll,
  It lives, and cannot die.

Fischer

1 When waves of trouble round me swell,
  My soul is not dismay'd;
I hear a voice I know full well,—
  "'T is I; be not afraid."

2 When black the threatening skies appear,
  And storms my path invade,
These accents tranquilize each fear,—
  "'T is I; be not afraid."

3 There is a gulf that must be cross'd;
  Saviour, be near to aid!
Whisper, when my frail bark is toss'd,—
  "'T is I; be not afraid."

4 There is a dark and fearful vale,
  Death hides within its shade;
O say, when flesh and heart shall fail,—
  "'T is I; be not afraid."

HOLLISTONE. C. M.

Let others boast how strong they be, | Nor death nor dan - ger fear;

But we'll con-fess, O Lord, to thee, | What fee-ble things we are.

VIOLA. C. M.

Arranged from
MENDELSSOHN.

I loved the Lord, he bowed his ear, | And chased my grief a - way: | O

let my heart no more despair, | While I have breath to pray.

1. Hap-py the heart where gra-ces reign, Where love in - spires the breast; Love

is the bright-est of the train, And strengthens all the rest, And

strengthens all the rest.

2 Knowledge, alas, 't is all in vain,
  And all in vain our fear;
Our stubborn sins will fight and reign,
  If love be absent there.

3 This is the grace that lives and sings,
  When faith and hope shall cease;
T'is this shall strike our joyful strings,
  In the sweet realms of bliss.

4 Before we quite forsake our clay,
  Or leave this dark abode,
The wings of love bear us away,
  To see our smiling God.

Holliston.

2 Fresh as the grass our bodies stand,
  And flourish bright and gay;
A blasting wind sweeps o'er the land,
  And fades the grass.

3 Our life contains a thousand springs,
  And dies, if one be gone;
Strange! that a harp of thousand strings
  Should keep in tune so long.

4 But 't is our God supports our frame,—
  The God who built us first;
Salvation to th' Almighty Name
  That reared us from the dust.

Viola.

2 From fear to hope, from hope to fear,
  My shipwrecked soul is tost,
Till I am tempted, in despair,
  To give up all for lost.

3 Yet through the stormy clouds I'll look
  Once more to Thee, my God;
O, fix my feet upon the rock,
  Beyond the raging flood,

4 One look of mercy from Thy face
  Will set my heart at ease;
One all-commanding word of grace
  Will make the tempest cease.

ABO. C. M. Double.

1. How love-ly are thy dwellings, Lord! From noise and trou-ble free; How
2. They pass refreshed the thirst-y vale, The dry and bar-ren ground, As

beau-ti-ful the sweet ac-cord Of souls that pray to thee! Lord
through a fruit-ful, wa-t'ry dale, Where springs and show'rs a-bound. They

God of Hosts, that reign'st on high! They are the tru-ly blest, Who
jour-ney on from strength to strength, With joy and gladsome cheer, Till

on-ly will on thee re-ly, In thee a-lone will rest.
all be-fore our God at length, In Zi-on's courts ap-pear.

1. Be - hold the west - ern even - ing light! It melts in deep - er gloom;
2. How beau-ti - ful on all the hill, The crim - son light is shed!

So calm the right - eous sink a - way, De - scend-ing to the tomb.
'Tis like the peace the dy - ing gives To mourners round his bed.

The winds breathe low—the yel - low leaf Scarce whis-pers from the tree!
How mild - ly on the wondering cloud The sun - set beam is cast!

So gent - ly flows the part - ing breath, When good men cease to be.
So sweet the memo - ry left be - hind, When loved ones breathe their last.

3 And lo! above the dews of night
  The vesper star appears!
So faith lights up the mourner's heart,
  Whose eyes are dim with tears.
Night falls, but soon the morning light
  Its glories shall restore;
And thus the eyes that sleep in death
  Shall wake, to close no more.

HARTFORD. C. M. Double.

Z.

1. O Lord, I would de - light in thee, And on thy care de - pend; To

thee in eve - ry trou - ble flee, My best, my on - ly friend. When

all cre - at - ed streams are dried, Thy ful - ness is the same; May

I with this be sat - is - fied, And glo - ry in thy name!

1. When, o - verwhelm'd with grief, My heart with - in me dies, Help-

2. O, lead me to the Rock That's hid a - bove my head, And

less, and far from all re - lief, To heaven I lift mine eyes, To

make the co - vert of Thy wings My shel - ter and my shade, My

heaven I lift mine eyes.

shel - ter and my shade.

3 Within Thy presence, Lord,
    For ever I'll abide;
Thou art the tower of my defence,
    The refuge where I hide.

4 Thou givest me the lot
    Of those that fear Thy name;
If endless life be their reward,
    I shall possess the same.

Hartford.

2 No good in creatures can be found,
    But may be found in Thee;
I must have all things, and abound,
    While God is God to me.
O Lord! I cast my care on Thee;
    I triumph and adore;
Henceforth my great concern shall be
    To love and please Thee more.

SONORA. S. M.

From lowest depths of woe, | To God I send my cry, | Lord, hear my suppli-

cating voice, | And gra - cious - ly reply, | And graciously re - ply.

PROVIDENCE. S. M.*

O Lord, our heavenly King, | Thy name is all di - vine; | Thy

glo - ries round the earth are spread, | And o'er the heavens they shine.

* NOTE. The third line may be sung by either Treble and Alto, or Tenor and Base, or all four parts in Unison.

SOLO—SOPRANO or TENOR.

1. Come to the land of peace, From sha - dows come a - way,
2. Come to the bright and blest, Gath - ered from ev - ery land;

Where all the sounds of weep - ing cease, And storms no more have sway.
For here thy soul shall find its rest, A - midst the shin - ing band.

TENOR.

Fear hath no dwell - ing here; But pure re - pose and love,
In this di - vine a - bode Change leaves no saddening trace;

Breathe

SOLO or QUARTETT.

Breathe thro' the bright, ce - les - tial air, The spir - it of the dove.
Come, trust - ing spir - it, to thy God, Thy ho - ly rest - ing - place.

through the bright,

SPRING. S. M. Double.

1. Thou gra-cious God and kind, O! cast our sins a-

way; Nor call our for - mer guilt to mind, Thy jus-tice to dis - play.

Spring.

2 Sweet is the dawn of day,
　When light just streaks the sky;
When shades and darkness pass away,
　And morning beams are nigh:
But sweeter far the dawn
　Of piety in youth;
When doubt and darkness are withdrawn,
　Before the light of truth.

3 Sweet is the early dew,
　Which gilds the mountain's tops,
And decks each plant and flower we view,
　With pearly glittering drops:
But sweeter far the scene
　On Zion's holy hill,
When there the dew of youth is seen
　Its freshness to distill.

Astoria.

1 Thou gracious God and kind,
　O! cast our sins away;
Nor call our former guilt to mind,
　Thy justice to display.

2 Thy tenderest mercies show,
　Thy richest grace prepare,
Ere yet, with guilty fears laid low,
　We perish in despair.

3 Save us from guilt and shame,
　Thy glory to display;
And, for the great Redeemer's name,
　Wash all our sins away.

3

NEWELL. S. M.

Z.

1. And must this bo - dy die? This mor - tal frame de - cay? And must these ac - tive

dim. et ritard.

limbs of mine Lie moldering in the clay? Lie moldering in the clay?

LOUISVILLE. S. M.

Z.

I stand on Zi-on's mount, And view my star-ry crown; No power on earth my

hope can shake, Nor hell can thrust me down, Nor hell can thrust me down.

1. Great is the Lord our God! And let his praise be great; He makes his church-es his a-bode, His most de-light-ful seat.

2 In Zion God is known—
   A refuge in distress;
 How bright has his salvation shone,
   Through all her palaces!

3 When kings against her joined,
   And saw the Lord was there;
 In wild confusion of the mind,
   They fled with hasty fear.

4 Oft have our fathers told,—
   Our eyes have often seen,—
 How well our God secures the fold
   Where his own sheep have been.

5 In every new distress,
   We'll to his house repair;
 We'll think upon his wond'rous grace,
   And seek deliverance there.

Newell.

1 And must this body die?—
   This mortal frame decay?
 And must these active limbs of mine
   Lie mouldering in the clay?

2 God, my Redeemer lives,
   And often from the skies
 Looks down and watches all my dust,—
   Till he shall bid it rise.

3 Arrayed in glorious grace,
   Shall these vile bodies shine;
 And every shape and every face,
   Look heavenly and divine.

4 These lively hopes we owe
   To Jesus' dying love;
 We would adore his grace below
   And sing his power above.

5 Dear Lord! accept the praise,
   Of these our humble songs;
 Till tunes of nobler sound we raise,
   With our immortal tongues.

Louisville.

1 I stand on Zion's mount,
   And view my starry crown;
 No power on earth my hope can shake,
   Nor hell can thrust me down.

2 The lofty hills and towers,
   That lift their heads on high;
 Shall all be leveled low in dust—
   Their very names shall die.

3 The vaulted heavens shall fall,
   Built by Jehovah's hands;
 But firmer than the heavens, the rock
   Of my salvation stands

1. Sol - diers of Christ! a - rise, And put your ar - mor on; Strong

in the strength which God sup - plies, Through his e - ter - nal Son; Strong

is the Lord of Hosts, And in his migh - ty power, Who

in the strength of Je - sus trusts, Is more than con - quer - or.

1. Je - sus, the Sa - vior's name, For - ev - er shall en - dure; Long

as the sun his matchless fame   Shall ev - er stand se - cure.

Cincinnati.

1 Soldiers of Christ, arise,
    And put your armor on,
Strong in the strength which God supplies
    Through his eternal Son;
Strong in the Lord of Hosts,
    And in his mighty power,
Who in the strength of Jesus trusts,
    Is more than conqueror.

2 From strength to strength go on;
    Wrestle, and fight, and pray;
Tread all the powers of darkness down,
    And win the well-fought day:
Still let the Spirit cry,
    In all his soldiers,—Come,
Till Christ the Lord descend from high,
    And take the conqu'rors home.

3 Stand then in his great might,
    With all his strength endued;
But take, to arm you for the fight,
    The panoply of God:
That having all things done,
    And all your conflicts past,
Ye may o'ercome, through Christ alone,
    And stand entire at last.

Niagara.

1 Jesus, the Savior's name
    Forever shall endure;
Long as the sun his matchless fame
    Shall ever stand secure.

2 Jehovah, God most high!
    We spread thy praise abroad;
Through the whole world thy fame shall fly
    O God, thine Israel's God!

3 Wonders of grace and power
    To thee alone belong;
Thy church those wonders shall adore,
    In everlasting song.

4 O Israel, bless him still,
    His name to honor raise;
Let the whole earth his glory fill,
    Mid songs of grateful praise.

5 Amen, our lips repeat,—
    Amen, we shout again:
Here all our wishes are complete,
    Let God our Savior reign!

1. Be - hold the day is come; The righteous Judge is near; And sinners, trembling

2. How aw - ful is the sight! How loud the thunders roar! The sun forbears to

at their doom, Shall soon their sentence hear. An - gels in bright at -

give his light, And stars are seen no more. The whole cre - a - tion

tire, Con - duct him through the skies; Dark - ness and tem - pest,

groans; But saints a - rise and sing: They are the ran - somed

smoke and fire, At - tend Him as He flies, At - tend Him as He flies.

of the Lord, And He their God and King, And He their God and King.

S. M. How swift the torrent rolls, | That bears us to the sea! | The
6s & 5s. 1. If life's pleasures charm thee, | Give them not thy heart,

tide that bears our tho'tless souls | To vast eter - ni - ty ! | Our fathers, where are
Lest the gift en - snare thee, | From thy God to part. | If distress be -

they, | With all they called their own? | Their joys, and griefs, and
- - fall thee, | Painful though it be, | Let not grief ap -

hopes and cares, | And wealth and honor gone.
- - pall thee, | To thy Saviour flee.

6s & 5s.

2. When earth's prospects fail thee,
  Let it not distress ;
Better comforts wait thee,
  Christ will freely bless.

3. Let not death alarm thee,
  Shrink not from his blow ;
For the conflict arm thee,
  Triumph o'er the foe.

WESLEY. S. M. Double.

1. Hark, how the watchmen cry! At - tend the trum - pet's sound; Stand
2. See on the mountain top The stan - dard of your God; In

to your arms, the foe is nigh.—The powers of hell sur - round. Who
Je - sus' name 't is lift - ed up, All stain'd with hallow'd blood. His

bow to Christ's com - mand, Your arms and hearts pre - pare; The
stan - dard - bear - ers, now To all the na - tion call: To

day of bat - tle is at hand,—Go forth to glo - rious war.
Je - sus' cross, ye na - tions, bow; He bore the cross for all.

3 Go up with Christ your Head ;
   Your Captain's footsteps see ;
Follow your Captain, and be led
   To certain victory.
All power to Him is given ;
   He ever reigns the same:
Salvation, happiness, and heaven,
   Are all in Jesus' name.

1. I was a wandering sheep, I did not love the fold: I did not love my
2. The Shepherd sought His sheep, The Father sought His child: They followed me o'er

Shepherd's voice, I would not be con - trolled; I was a wayward child, I
vale and hill, O'er des - erts waste and wild: They found me nigh to death, Fam-

did not love my home, I did not love my Father's voice, I loved a - far to roam.
ish'd, and faint, and lone; They bound me with the bands of love, They saved the wand'ring one.

3 They spoke in tender love,
   They raised my drooping head;
They gently closed my bleeding wounds,
   My fainting soul they fed:
They washed my filth away,
   They made me clean and fair;
They brought me to my home in peace,
   The long-sought wanderer.

4 Jesus my shepherd is,
   'T was He that loved my soul,
'T was He that wash'd me in His blood,
   'T was He that made me whole:

'T was He that sought the lost,
   That found the wandering sheep,
'T was He that brought me to the fold—
   'T is He that still doth keep.

5 No more a wand'ring sheep,
   I love to be controll'd,
I love my tender Shepherd's voice,
   I love the peaceful fold:
No more a wayward child,
   I seek no more to roam,
I love my heavenly Father's voice—
   I love, I love His home.

Z.

O God!—my gra-cious God— to thee My morning prayers shall of - fered be; For

thee my thirs-ty soul doth pant; My faint-ing flesh im-plores thy grace, With -

in this dry and bar - ren place, Where I re-fresh-ing wa - ters want.

1 O God!—my gracious God—to thee
  My morning prayers shall offered be ;
    For thee my thirsty soul doth pant ;
  My fainting flesh implores thy grace,
  Within this dry and barren place,
    Where I refreshing waters want.

2 O to my longing eyes once more
  That view of glorious power restore,
    Which thy majestic house displays !
  Because to me thy wondrous love
  Than life itself does dearer prove,
    My lips shall always speak thy praise.

1. O Thou that hear'st the prayer of faith, Wilt thou not save a
soul from death, That casts it-self on thee? I have no ref - uge
of my own, But fly to what my Lord hath done, And suf-fered once for
me, And suf-fered once for me.

2.

Then save me from eternal death,
The spirit of adoption breathe,
  His consolations send;
By him some word of life impart,
And sweetly whisper to my heart,
  "Thy Maker is thy Friend."

3.

The king of terrors then would be
A welcome messenger to me
  To bid me come away:
Unclogged by earth, or earthly things,
I'd mount, I'd fly, with eager wings,
  To everlasting day.

The songs of Zi - on oft im - part, To each poor,

laboring, care-worn heart, The balm of heavenly peace ; They chase a -

- - way each bod - ing fear, And turn to joy each sorrowing

fear, And bid the tu - mult cease, And bid the tu - mult cease.

1. The mighty God who rolls the spheres, And storm, and fire, and hail prepares, And

guides this vast ma-chine; His powerful hand our life sus - tains, And

scat - ters all those joys and pains That fill this checkered scene.

That fill this checkered scene.

2 His piercing eye at once surveys
   Where thousand suns and systems blaze,
      And where the sparrow falls;
   While seraphs tune their harps on high,
   His ear attends the softest cry,
      When human misery calls.

3 Eternal God! who shall not fear,
   And trust, and love with soul sincere,
      Thy awful, glorious name?
   While man, Thy creature, swift decays,
   Time has no measure for Thy days,
      Nor limit for Thy fame.

1. Blow ye the trumpet!—blow,—The gladly solemn sound! Let all the na-tions know, To

2. Ex-alt the Lamb of God,—The sin-a-ton-ing Lamb; Redemp-tion by his blood, Through

earth's re-mot-est bound,—The year of ju-bi-lee is come; Re-

all the world pro-claim; The year of ju-bi-lee is come; Re-

turn, ye ran-somed sin-ners! home, Re-turn, ye ran-somed sin-ners! home.

turn, ye ran-somed sin-ners! home, Re-turn, ye ran-somed sin-ners! home.

3 Ye slaves of sin and hell!
Your liberty receive;
And safe in Jesus dwell,
And blest in Jesus live:
The year of jubilee is come;
Return, ye ransomed sinners! home.
(10)

4 The gospel-trumpet hear,
The news of pardoning grace;
Ye happy souls! draw near,
Behold your Savior's face:
The year of jubilee is come;
Return, ye ransomed sinners! home.

1 How pleas-ing is thy voice, O Lord, our heaven-ly King, That

2. The morn with glo-ry crowned, Thy hand ar-rays in smiles; Thou

bids the frosts re--tire, And wakes the love-ly spring! The

bid'st the eve de--cline, Re-joic-ing, o'er the hills. Soft

rains re-turn, the ice dis-tils, And plains and hills for-get to mourn

suns as-cend, the mild wind blows, And beau-ty glows to earth's far end.

3 Thou mak'st the pastures green,
    Thou call'st the flocks abroad,
The springing corn proclaims
    The footsteps of our God:
        Both bird and beast
        Partake thy care,
        And happy, share
    The general feast.

4 The thunder is his voice,
    His arrows blazing fires;
He glows in yonder sun,
    And smiles in starry choirs:
        The balmy breeze
        His breath perfumes,
        His beauty blooms
    In flowers and trees.

O Zi - on! tune thy voice, And raise thy hands on high; Tell all the earth thy joys, And boast sal - va - tion nigh: Cheerful in God, A - rise and shine, While rays di - vine Stream all a-broad, While rays di - vine Stream all a - broad.

1 O Zion! tune thy voice,
    And raise thy hands on high;
Tell all the earth thy joys,
    And boast salvation nigh:
      Cheerful in God,
        Arise and shine,
      While rays divine
    Stream all abroad.

2 He gilds thy mourning face
    With beams that cannot fade;
His all-resplendent grace
    He pours around thy head;
      The nations round
        Thy form shall view,
      With lustre new
    Divinely crowned.

3 In honor to his name,
    Reflect that sacred light;
And loud that grace proclaim
    Which makes thy darkness bright;
      Pursue his praise,
        Till sovereign love,
      In worlds above,
    The glory raise.

4 There, on his holy hill,
    A brighter sun shall rise,
And, with his radiance, fill
    Those fairer, purer skies;
      While, round his throne,
        Ten thousand stars,
      In nobler spheres,
    His influence own.

1. Come, every pi-ous heart, That loves the Savior's name! Your noblest powers ex-ert, To cel-e-brate his fame; Tell all a-bove, and all be-low, The debt of love to him you owe, The debt of love to him you owe.

1 Come, every pious heart,
  That loves the Savior's name!
Your noblest powers exert
  To celebrate his fame;
Tell all above, and all below,
The debt of love to him you owe.

2 He left his starry crown,
  And laid his robes aside,
On wings of love came down,
  And wept, and bled, and died:
What he endured, no tongue can tell,
To save our souls from death and hell!

3 From the dark grave he rose—
  The mansion of the dead;
And thence his mighty foes
  In glorious triumph led:
Up through the sky the conqueror rode,
And reigns on high, the Savior—God.

4 From thence he'll quickly come,—
  His chariot will not stay,—
And bear our spirits home
  To realms of endless day:
There shall we see his lovely face,
And ever be in his embrace.

RAYMOND. 7s. (DOUBLE.)

Source of be - ing, source of light, | With un - fad - ing beau - ties

bright; | Thee, when morning greets the skies, | Blushing sweet with humid

eyes; | Thee, when soft de - clin - ing day | Sinks in pur - ple waves a -

- way; | Thee, O Pa - rent, will I sing, | To thy feet my tribute bring!

1. In the sun, and moon, and stars, | Signs and wonders there shall
2. E - vil thoughts shall shake the proud, | Racking doubt and restless

be ; | Earth shall quake with in - ward wars, | Nations with per - plex - i -
fear ; | And a - mid the thunder - cloud | Shall the Judge of men ap -

- ty. | Soon shall o - cean's hoary deep, | Tossed with stronger tem - pests,
- pear. | But tho' from that aw - ful face | Heaven shall fade, and earth shall

rise ; | Darker storms the mountain sweep, | Redder lightning rend the skies.
fly, | Fear not ye, his chosen race, | Your re - demption draweth nigh!

KIDRON. 7s. Double.

1. 'Tis my hap-pi-ness be-low, Not to live with-out the cross,

2. God, in Is-rael, sows the seeds Of af-flic-tion, pain, and toil;

But the Sav-iour's power to know, Sanc-ti-fy-ing eve-ry loss.

These spring up, and choke the weeds Which would else o'erspread the soil.

Duet or Terzet.

Tri-als must and will be-fall; But, with hum-ble faith to see

Tri-als make the prom-ise sweet; Tri-als give new life to prayer;

Love inscribed up-on them all— This is hap-pi-ness to me.

Tri-als bring me to his feet— Lay me low, and keep me there.

As the hart, with ea-ger looks, Pant-eth for the wa-ter brooks,
So my soul, a-thirst for thee, Pants the liv-ing God to see;

When, O when, with fil-ial fear, Lord, shall I to thee draw near?

Lord, shall I to thee draw near?

2.
Why art thou cast down, my soul?
God, thy God, shall make thee whole;
Why art thou disquieted?
God shall lift thy fallen head,
And his countenance benign
Be the saving health of thine.

1 Holy Spirit! Lord of light!
From thy clear celestial height,
Come, thou Light of all that live!
Thy pure beaming radiance give.

2 Come, thou Father of the poor!
Come with treasures that endure;
Thou, of all consolers best,
Visiting the troubled breast.

3 Thou in toil art comfort sweet;
Pleasant coolness in the heat;
Solace in the midst of woe;
Dost refreshing peace bestow.

4 Light immortal! Light divine!
Visit thou these hearts of thine;
If thou take thy grace away,
Nothing pure in man will stay.

5 Heal our wounds—our strength renew;
On our dryness pour thy dew;
Wash the stains of guilt away;
Guide the steps that go astray.

6 Give us comfort when we die;
Give us life with thee on high;
In thy sevenfold gifts descend;
Give us joys which never end.

* First published in Plymouth Collection.

* In 7s single omit the repeat.

MARY. 7s. (DOUBLE.)

Jesus, lov-er of my soul, | Let me to thy bosom fly; | Let the billows near me

Hide me, O my Sa-viour, hide, | Till the

Hide me, O my Saviour, hide,

roll, | While the tempest still is high: | Hide me, O my Saviour, hide, | Till the

Hide me, O my Saviour, hide,

storm of life is past; | Safe in-to the haven guide;

Till the storm of life is past, | Safe into the haven guide;

storm of life is past; | Safe in-to the haven guide; | O receive my soul at last.

Till the storm of life is past, | Safe into the haven guide;

1. Soft - ly fades the twi - light ray Of the ho - ly Sab - bath day;
2. Night her sol - emn man - tle spreads O'er the earth as day - light fades;

Gent - ly as life's set - ting sun, When the Christian's
All things tell of calm re - pose At the ho - ly

course is run, When the Chris - tian's course is run.
Sab - bath's close, At the ho - ly Sab - bath's close.

Mary.

2 Other refuge have I none—
Hangs my helpless soul on Thee;
Leave, ah! leave me not alone,
Still support and comfort me;
All my trust on Thee is stayed,
All my hopes from Thee I bring;
Cover my defenceless head
With the shadow of thy wing.

3 Thou, O Christ, art all I want,
Boundless love in Thee I find,
Raise the fallen, cheer the faint,
Heal the sick, and lead the blind.
Just and holy is Thy name,
I am all unrighteousness;
Vile and full of sin I am—
Thou art full of truth and grace.

4 Plenteous grace with Thee is found—
Grace to pardon all my sin ;
Let the healing streams abound,
Make and keep me pure within;

Thou of life the fountain art,
Freely let me take of Thee;
Spring Thou up within my heart,
Rise to all eternity.

Edith.

3 Peace is on the world abroad;
'Tis the holy peace of God—
Symbol of the peace within,
When the spirit rests from sin.

4 Still the Spirit lingers near,
Where the evening worshipper
Seeks communion with the skies,
Pressing onward to the prize.

5 Saviour, may our Sabbaths be
Days of peace and joy to Thee,
Till in heaven our souls repose,
Where the Sabbath ne'er shall close.

Jesus, lov - er   of   my soul, | Let me to   thy bo-som fly, | While the

billows near me roll, | While the tempest still is high : | Hide me, O my Saviour,

hide, | Till the storm of life   is   past ; | Safe in - to   the ha - ven

Other Ending.

guide ; | O receive   my soul at last, | O   re-ceive my soul at last.

1. Songs of praise the an - gels sang, Heaven with hal - le - lu - jahs rang,

Heaven with hal-le - lu-jahs rang,

When Je - ho - vah's work be - gun, When he spake, and it was done.

When he spake, and it was done.

Ilsley.

1 Songs of praise the angels sang,
Heaven with hallelujahs rang,
When Jehovah's work begun,
When he spake, and it was done.

2 Songs of praise awoke the morn,
When the Prince of peace was born;
Songs of praise arose, when he
Captive led captivity.

3 Heaven and earth must pass away,—
Songs of praise shall crown that day:
God will make new heavens and earth,
Songs of praise shall hail their birth.

4 And shall man alone be dumb,
Till that glorious morning come?
No!—the church delights to raise
Psalms, and hymns, and songs of praise.

5 Saints below, with heart and voice,
Still in songs of praise rejoice,
Learning here, by faith and love,
Songs of praise to sing above.

6 Borne upon their latest breath,
Songs of praise shall conquer death;
Then, amid eternal joy,
Songs of praise their powers employ

OBERLIN. 7s Double.

ANDANTE.

1 An-gel, roll the rock a-way! Death, yield up thy mighty prey! See! he ris-es

from the tomb, Glow-ing with im - mor-tal bloom! 'Tis the Sa - vior,
'Tis the Savior,
'Tis the Sa - vior,

An - gel, raise Shouts of ev - er - last . . . ing praise! Let the world's re
Shouts of ev - er - last-ing praise!
An - gel, raise Shouts of ev - er - last - - ing praise!

motest bound, Hear the joy-in-spir-ing sound, Hear the joy-in-spir-ing sound.

1. Now be - gin the heavenly theme! Sing a - loud in Je - sus' name!

Ye who his sal - va - tion prove, Tri - umph in re - deem - ing love.

Oberlin.

2 'Tis the Savior! Angel, raise
Shouts of everlasting praise:
Let the world's remotest bound
Hear the joy-inspiring sound.

2 Saints on earth, lift up your eyes,—
Now to glory see him rise
In long triumph through the sky,
Up to waiting worlds on high.

3 Heaven unfolds its portals wide!
Mighty conqueror! through them ride;
King of glory! mount thy throne,
Boundless empire is thine own.

5 Powers of heaven, seraphic choirs,
Sing, and sweep your golden lyres;
Sons of men, in humbler strain,
Sing your mighty Savior's reign.

6 Every note with wonder swell,
Sin o'erthrown, and captive hell!
Where, O death, is now thy sting?
Where thy terrors, vanquished king?

Indianopolis.

2 Ye, who see the Father's grace
Beaming in the Savior's face,
As to Canaan on ye move,
Praise and bless redeeming love,

3 Mourning souls! dry up your tears,
Banish all your sinful fears;
See your guilt and curse remove.
Cancelled by redeeming love.

4 Welcome all, by sin oppressed,—
Welcome to his sacred rest!
Nothing brought him from above,—
Nothing but redeeming love.

5 Hither, then, your music bring;
Strike aloud each joyful string;
Mortals! join the hosts above,—
Join to praise redeeming love.

6 When his Spirit leads us home,
When we to his glory come,
We shall all the fulness prove
Of the Lord's redeeming love.

LAFON. 7s.

Z.

Je - sus! Lord! we look to thee! Let us in thy name a - gree;

Show thy - self the Prince of peace, Bid all strife for - ev - er cease.

NEWARK. 7s.

Z.

Depth of mer-cy!—Can there be Mer-cy still reserved for me? Can my

God his wrath for - bear. And the chief of sin - ners spare?

Arranged from Mendelssohn. Z.

1. Could my heart so hard re - main, Prayer a task and burden prove, Eve - ry

tri - fle give me pain, If I knew a Sa - vior's love?

If I knew a Sa - vior's love?

2 If I pray, or hear, or read,
  Sin is mixed with all I do;
  You who love the Lord indeed,
  Tell me—is it thus with you?

3 Yet I mourn my stubborn will,
  Find my sin a grief and thrall;
  Should I grieve for what I feel,
  If I did not love at all?

4 Lord, decide the doubtful case—
  Thou who art thy people's sun,
  Shine upon thy work of grace,
  If it be indeed begun.

5 Let me love thee more and more,
  If I love at all, I pray;
  If I have not loved before,
  Help me to begin to-day.

Lafon.

1 Jesus, Lord! we look to thee!
  Let us in thy name agree;
  Show thyself the Prince of peace,
  Bid all strife forever cease.

2 Make us one in heart and mind,
  Courteous, pitiful and kind,
  Lowly, meek, in thought and word,
  Wholly like our blessed Lord.

3 Let us each for others care,
  Each his brother's burthen bear,
  To thy church a pattern give,
  Showing how believers live.

4 Let us then with joy remove
  To thy family above;
  On the wings of angels fly,—
  Showing how believers die.

Newark.

1 Depth of mercy!—can there be
  Mercy still reserved for me?
  Can my God his wrath forbear,
  And the chief of sinners spare?

2 I have long withstood his grace,
  Long provoked him to his face;
  Would not hear his gracious calls;
  Grieved him by a thousand falls.

3 Jesus, answer from above;
  Is not all thy nature love?
  Wilt thou not the wrong forget—
  Lo, I fall before thy feet.

4 Now incline me to repent;
  Let me now my fall lament;
  Deeply my revolt deplore,
  Weep, believe, and sin no more.

WATCHMAN. 7s.

Watchman! tell us of the night, | What its signs of pro - mise are—

Traveler! o'er yon mountain's height, | See that glo - ry - beam - ing star!

Soli.

Watchman! does its beauteous ray | Aught of joy or hope foretell?

Tutti. *ff*

Traveler! yes; it brings the day— | Promised day of Is - ra - el.

* May be used as a single 7s from the beginning to the *. This tune requires an exceedingly delicate execution,—Double Quartette will do best for it.

1. Breth-ren, while we so-journ here, Fight we must, but should not fear;
2. In the way a thou-sand snares Lie, to take us un-a-wares;

Foes we have, but we've a Friend, One that loves us to the end.
Sa-tan, with ma-li-cious art, Watch-es each un-guard-ed part:

For-ward, then, with cour-age go, Long we shall not dwell be-low;
But, from Sa-tan's mal-ice free, Saints shall soon vic-to-rious be;

Soon the joy-ful news will come, "Child, your Fa-ther calls—come home."
Soon the joy-ful news will come, "Child, your Fa-ther calls—come home."

Watchman.

3 Watchman! tell us of the night,
   For the morning seems to dawn,—
Traveler! darkness takes its flight,
   Doubt and terror are withdrawn.
Watchman! let thy wanderings cease;
   Hie thee to thy quiet home.
Traveler! lo! the Prince of Peace,
   Lo! the Son of God is come!

3 But of all the foes we meet
   None so oft mislead our feet,
None betray us into sin,
   Like the foes that dwell within;
Yet let nothing spoil our peace,
   Christ shall also conquer these;
Soon the joyful news will come,
   "Child, your Father calls—come home!"

VINTON. 7s. Double.

Arranged. 2

1. Lord! we come before thee now; At thy feet we humbly bow; Oh! do
not our suit disdain! Shall we seek thee, Lord in vain! Lord on thee our souls depend.

Cres - cen -

do. In compassion now descend; Fill our hearts with thy rich

grace. Tune our lips to sing thy praise.

2 In thine own appointed way,
Now we seek thee, here we stay;
Lord! we know not how to go,
Till a blessing thou bestow.
Send some message from thy word,
That may joy and peace afford;
Let thy Spirit now impart
Full salvation to each heart.

3 Comfort those who weep and mourn;
Let the time of joy return:
Those who are cast down, lift up;
Make them strong in faith and hope.
Grant that all may seek and find
Thee, a God supremely kind:
Heal the sick, the captive free;
Let us all rejoice in thee.

1. Hap - py soul, thy days are end - ing, All thy mourn-ing
2. For the joy he sets be - fore thee, Bear a mo - men-

days be - low; Go,—the an - gel guards at - tend - ing.—To the
ta - ry pain; Die, to live a life of glo - ry; Suf - fer,.

sight of Je - sus go. Waiting to receive thy spi - rit, Lo! the
with thy Lord to reign. Struggle through thy lat-est pas - sion, To thy

Sav - ior stands a - bove; Shows the ful - ness of his mer - it, Reaches
great Re-deem-er's breast, To his ut - ter-most sal - va - tion, To his

out the crown of love, Reaches out the crown of love.
e - ver-last-ing rest, To his e - ver - last - ing rest.

MOUNT ZION. 8s & 7s. (Double.)

Arranged from a Cantata for male voices, composed by J. ZUNDEL.

1. Glo - rious things of thee are spo-ken, Zi - on, ci - ty of our God!
He whose word can - not be bro-ken, Form'd thee for his own a - bode,

On the rock of a - ges found - ed, What can shake thy sure re - pose?

With sal - va - tion's walls sur - round-ed, Thou may'st smile at all thy foes.

Thou may'st smile at all thy foes.

2 See, the streams of living waters,
  Springing from eternal love,
Well supply thy sons and daughters,
  And all fear of want remove:
Who can faint while such a river
  Ever flows thy thirst t' assuage?
Grace, which like the Lord, the giver,
  Never fails from age to age.

3 Round each habitation hovering,
  See the cloud and fire appear!
For a glory and a covering,
  Showing that the Lord is near:—
He who gives them daily manna,
  He who listens when they cry,
Let him hear the loud hosanna
  Rising to his throne on high

Choral   Z.

1. Know, my soul, thy full sal - va - tion; Rise o'er sin, and fear, and care;
   Joy to   find, in eve - ry sta - tion, Something still to   do   or   bear.

Think what Spi - rit dwells with - in thee; Think what Father's smiles are   thine; Think that

Je - sus died to   win thee: Child of heav'n, canst thou   re - pine?

1 Know, my soul, thy full salvation;
   Rise o'er sin, and fear, and care;
Joy to find, in every station,
   Something still to do or bear.
Think what Spirit dwells within thee;
   Think what Father's smiles are thine,
Think that Jesus died to win thee:
   Child of heaven, canst thou repine?

2 Haste thee on from grace to glory,
   Armed by faith, and winged by prayer!
Heaven's eternal day 's before thee;
   God's own hand shall guide thee there. .
Soon shall close thy earthly mission,
   Soon shall pass thy pilgrim days;
Hope shall change to glad fruition,
   Faith to sight, and prayer to praise.

Arranged. Z.

7s 6 lines. Hearken, Lord, to my com-plaints, For my soul with-in me faints;

8s & 7s. Light of those whose dreary dwelling Bor - ders on the shades of death!
Come, and by thy love re - vealing, Dis - si - pate the clouds be - neath:

Thee, far off, I call to mind, In the land I left be - hind;

The new heaven and earth's Cre - ator, In our deep - est dark - ness rise,

Where the streams of Jor - dan flow, Where the heights of Her - mon glow.

Scat - t'ring all the night of nature, Pour - ing eye - sight on our eyes.

1. Lo! the Lord Je-ho-vah liv-eth! He's my rock, I bless his name: He, my God, sal-va-tion giv-eth; All ye lands, ex-alt his fame.

Esther. 7s.

1 Hearken, Lord, to my complaints,
For my soul within me faints;
Thee, far off, I call to mind,
In the land I left behind,
Where the streams of Jordan flow,
Where the heights of Hermon glow.

2 Tempest-tost, my failing bark
Founders on the ocean dark ;
Deep to deep around me calls,
With the rush of waterfalls,
While I plunge to lower caves,
Overwhelmed by all thy waves.

3 Once the morning's earliest light
Brought thy mercy to my sight,
And my wakeful song was heard
Later than the evening bird ;
Hast thou all my prayers forgot ?
Dost thou scorn, or hear them not ?

4 Why, my soul, art thou perplexed ?
Why with faithless troubles vexed ?
Hope in God, whose saving name
Thou shalt joyfully proclaim,
When his countenance shall shine
Through the clouds that darken thine.

Esther. 8s & 7s.

1 Light of those whose dreary dwelling
Borders on the shades of death !
Come, and, by thy love revealing,
Dissipate the clouds beneath :

The new heaven and earth's Creator,
In our deepest darkness rise,
Scattering all the night of nature,
Pouring eyesight on our eyes.

2 Still we wait for thine appearing;
Life and joy thy beams impart,
Chasing all our fears, and cheering
Every poor, benighted heart:
Come, and manifest thy favor
To the ransomed, helpless race ;
Come, thou glorious God and Saviour,
Come, and bring the gospel grace.

Anthony.

1 Lo! the Lord Jehovah liveth!
He's my rock, I bless his name;
He, my God, salvation giveth—
All ye lands, exalt his fame.

2 O'er his enemies exalted,
See the great Redeemer rise!
Though by powers of hell assaulted,
God supports him to the skies.

3 God, Messiah's cause maintaining,
Shall his righteous throne extend,
O'er the world the Saviour reigning,
Earth shall at his footstool bend.

Call Je - ho - vah thy sal - va - tion; | Rest beneath th' Almighty's shade;

In his sa - cred hab - i - ta - tion, | Dwell, nor ev - er be dismayed:

There no tu - mult can a - larm thee, | Thou shalt dread no hid - den snare;

Guile nor vi - o - lence can harm thee, | In e - ter - nal safe-guard there.

1. Father, they who Thee receive, And in Thee begin to live,

Alto Solo.

2. Fix, O, fix my wavering mind! To the cross my spirit bind:

Day and night they cry to Thee, As Thou art, so let us be.

Earthly passions far remove; Fill the soul with perfect love.

As Thou art so let us be.

Fill the soul with perfect love.

3 Who in heart on Thee believes,
He the promise now receives;
He with joy beholds Thy face,
Triumphs in Thy pardoning grace.

4 Boundless wisdom, power divine,
Love unspeakable, art Thine:
Praise by all to Thee be given,
Sons of earth and hosts of heaven.

Stuttgart.

2 From the sword, at noonday wasting,
  From the noisome pestilence,
In the depth of midnight, blasting,
  God shall be thy sure defence.
Fear not thou the deadly quiver,
  When a thousand feel the blow;
Mercy shall thy soul deliver,
  Though ten thousand be laid low.

3 Since, with pure and firm affection,
  Thou on God hast set thy love,
With the wings of His protection
  He will shield thee from above;
Thou shalt call on Him in trouble,
  He will hearken, He will save;
Here, for grief, reward thee double,
  Crown with life beyond the grave.

LIFE'S BILLOWS. 8s & 7s Double.

Z.

1. Tossed up-on life's rag-ing bil-low, Sweet it is, O Lord, to know,

Thou didst press a sail-or's pil-low, And canst feel a sail-or's woe.

Nev-er slumbering, nev-er sleep-ing, Though the night be dark and drear,

Thou the faith-ful watch art keeping; "All, all 's well!" thy con-stant cheer.

1. Sa - vior! breathe an eve-ning blessing, Ere re - pose our spi-rits seal;

Sin and want we come con - fess-ing; Thou canst save and thou canst heal.

Life's Billows.

1 Toss'd upon life's raging billow,
  Sweet it is, O Lord, to know
Thou didst press a sailor's pillow,
  And canst feel a sailor's woe.
Never slumbering, never sleeping,
  Though the night be dark and drear,
Thou the faithful watch art keeping,
  "All, all's well," thy constant cheer.

2 And though loud the wind is howling,
  Fierce though flash the lightnings red;
Darkly, though the storm-cloud's scowling
  O'er the sailor's anxious head;
Thou canst calm the raging ocean,
  All its noise and tumult still,
Hush the tempest's wild commotion,
  At the bidding of thy will.

3 Thus my heart the hope will cherish,
  While to thee I lift mine eye;
Thou wilt save me ere I perish,
  Thou wilt hear the sailor's cry.
And though mast and sail be riven,
  Life's short voyage will soon be o'er;
Safely moor'd in heaven's wide haven,
  Storm and tempest vex no more.

Milwaukee.

1 Savior! breathe an evening blessing,
  Ere repose our spirits seal;
Sin and want we come confessing;
  Thou canst save, and thou canst heal.

2 Though destruction walk around us,
  Though the arrows past us fly,
Angel-guards from thee surround us;
  We are safe, if thou art nigh.

3 Though the night be dark and dreary,
  Darkness cannot hide from thee;
Thou art he, who, never weary,
  Watcheth where thy people be.

4 Should swift death this night o'ertake us,
  And our couch become our tomb,
May the morn in heaven awake us,
  Clad in bright and deathless bloom.

———

DEVOTION. 8s. & 7s. (Double.)

FOR QUARTET OR SMALL CHOIRS.

Z.

Love di-vine. all love ex - cell - ing! Joy of heaven, to earth come down! Fix in

f Treble Solo.

us thy hum - ble dwell-ing, All thy faith - ful mer-cies crown, Je - sus!

Organ.

Chorus. Tenor. Cres - - cen - -

thou art all com-passion! Pure, un - bound-ed love thou art; Vis - it us with thy sal -

do. *f* *pp*

va - tion. En - ter ev' - ry trembling heart, En - ter ev' - ry trembling heart.

Z.

1. Part-ing soul, the floods a - wait thee, And the bil-lows round thee roar; Yet re-

joice; the ho - ly ci - ty Stands on yon ce - les - tial shore.

1 Parting soul, the floods await thee,
    And the billows round thee roar;
  Yet rejoice; the holy city
  ' Stands on yon celestial shore.

2 There are crowns and thrones of glory,
    There the living waters glide;
  There the just in shining raiment,
    Standing by Immanuel's side.

3 Linger not, the stream is narrow,
    Though its cold dark waters rise;
  He who passed the flood before thee,
    Guides thy path to yonder skies.

Devotion.

1 Love divine, all love excelling,—
    Joy of heaven, to earth come down!
  Fix in us thy humble dwelling,
    All thy faithful mercies crown.

Jesus! thou art all compassion,
    Pure, unbounded love thou art;
  Visit us with thy salvation,
    Enter every trembling heart.

2 Breathe!—Oh! breathe thy loving Spirit
    Into every troubled breast;
  Let us all thy grace inherit,
    Let us find thy promised rest:
  Take away the love of sinning,
    Take our load of guilt away;
  End the work of thy beginning,—
    Bring us to eternal day.

3 Carry on thy new creation,
    Pure and holy may we be;
  Let us see our whole salvation
    Perfectly secured by thee;
  Change from glory into glory,
    Till in heaven we take our place;
  Till we cast our crowns before thee,
    Lost in wonder, love, and praise.

NEW HAVEN. 8s & 7s Double.

Z.

1. O my God, by thee for - sak - en, Pros-trate in the dust I
2. Deep to deep re-spon-sive call - ing, Thunders roar, the tor - rents

lie; Faith by gloom-y ter - rors shak - en, All my hopes with-in me
roll; Burst-ing clouds a - round me fall - ing, Wave on wave o'erwhelms my

die: Yet my soul, in thee con - fid - ing, Me - di - tates thy mer - cy
soul: Yet the Lord, his grace com - mand - ing, Will with mer - cies crown my

still; Tho' on earth's dark coast a - bid - ing, Dis - tant far from Zi - on's hill.
days: He my guard-ian, near me stand - ing, Cheers my nights with prayer and praise.

1. Love di - vine, all love ex - cell - ing, Joy of heaven, to earth come down!

Fix in us thy hum - ble dwelling, All Thy faith - ful mer - cies crown.

Je - sus Thou art all com - pas - sion, Pure, unbound - ed love Thou art;

Vis - it us with Thy sal - va - tion, En - ter eve - ry trembling heart.

2 Breathe, O breathe Thy loving Spirit
　Into every troubled breast!
Let us all in Thee inherit,
　Let us find Thy promised rest.
Come, Almighty to deliver,
　Let us all Thy grace receive!
Suddenly return, and never,
　Never more Thy temples leave!

3 Finish then Thy new creation,
　Pure, and spotless may we be;
Let us see our whole salvation
　Perfectly secured by Thee!
Changed from glory into glory,
　Till in heaven we take our place;
Till we cast our crowns before Thee,
　Lost in wonder, love, and praise.

SYRACUSE. 8s & 7s Double.

Z.

1. Come, thou fount of ev'ry blessing, Tune my heart to sing thy grace:
Streams of mer-cy, nev-er ceas-ing, Call for songs of (omit.)

loud-est praise. Teach me some me-lo-dious son-net, Sung by flam-ing

tongues a-bove: Praise the mount—I'm fixed up-on it;

Mount of thy re-deem-ing love! Mount of thy re-deem-ing love!

Z.

1. Gent - ly, Lord! O gent - ly lead us Through this lone - ly vale of

2. In the hour of pain and an - guish, In the hour when death draws

tears; Through the chan - ges thou'st de - creed us, Till our last great change ap -

near, Suf - fer not our hearts to lan-guish, Suf - fer not our souls to

p Soli

pears: When temp - ta - tion's darts as - sail us, When in de - vious paths we

p

fear; And, when mor - tal life is end - ed, Bid us on thy bo - som

p

p Chorus.   *ff*

stray, Let thy good-ness nev - er fail us, Lead us in thy per - fect way.

p   *ff*

rest, Till, by an - gel - bands at - tend - ed, We a - wake a - mong the blest.

ff

Solo.

1. Come to Cal - vary's ho - ly moun-tain, Sin - ners, ru - ined by the fall!

Organ or Piano.

f

Here a pure and heal - ing foun - tain Flows to you, to me, to all,

f

Chorus.

In a full, per - pet - ual tide, O - pened when our Sa - vior died,

Soli.

p

Chorus.

O - pened when our Sa - vior died.

2 Come, in sorrow and contrition,
    Wounded, impotent, and blind!
  Here the guilty, free remission,
    Here the troubled, peace may find;
  Health this fountain will restore;
  He that drinks shall thirst no more

3 He that drinks shall live forever:
    'Tis a soul-renewing flood;
  God is faithful; God will never
    Break his covenant in blood,
  Signed when our Redeemer died,
  Sealed when he was glorified.

Z.

1. Men of God, go take your sta-tions, Dark-ness reigns throughout the earth;

Go, pro-claim a-mong the na-tions, Joy-ful news of heaven-ly birth:

Bear the ti-dings—Bear the ti-dings—Ti-dings of the Sa-vior's worth.

2 Of his gospel not ashamed,—
   'T is the power of God to save;
Go where Christ was never named,
   Publish freedom to the slave :
      Blessed freedom !
   Freedom Zion's children have.
      (14)

3 When exposed to fearful dangers,
   Jesus will his own defend ;
Borne afar midst foes and strangers,
   Jesus will appear your friend :
      He is with you,—
   He will guide you to the end.

WELCOME. 8s, 7s & 4s.

1. Welcome, wel-come, dear Re - deem - er, Wel - come to this heart of mine;

Lord, I make a full sur - ren - der, Eve - ry power and thought be thine;

Thine en - tire - ly, Thine en - tire - ly, Through e - ter - nal a - ges thine.

1 Welcome, welcome, dear Redeemer,
   Welcome to this heart of mine;
Lord, I make a full surrender,
   Every power and thought be thine;
     Thine entirely,
   T' ugh eternal ages thine.

2 Known to all to be thy mansion,
   Earth and hell will disappear;
Or in vain attempt possession,
   When they find the Lord is near—
     Shout, O Zion!
   Shout, ye saints, the Lord is here!

1. Lord I dis-miss us with thy bless-ing, Fill our hearts with joy and peace;

Let us each, thy love pos-sess-ing, Tri-umph in re-deem-ing grace;

O re-fresh us, O re-fresh us, Trav'-ling through this wil-der-ness.

2 Thanks we give and adoration,
　For thy gospel's joyful sound;
May the fruits of thy salvation
　In our hearts and lives abound
　　May thy presence
　With us evermore be found.

3 So, whene'er the signal's given
　Us from earth to call away,
Borne on angel's wings to heaven
　Glad the summons to obey,
　　May we ever
　Reign with Christ in endless day.

ANTIPHONAL TUNE. 8s, 7s & 4s.

J. ZUNDEL.

Lo! he comes, with clouds des - cend-ing, Once for fa - vor'd sin - ners slain : Swell the tri-umph of his

Thousand, thousand saints at - tend-ing, Swell the tri-umph of his

train. Hal - le - lu - jah! Hal - le - lu - jah! Je - sus Christ shall ev - er

train. Hal - le - lu - jah! Hal - le - lu - jah! Je - sus Christ shall ev - er

reign! Hal - le - lu - jah, Hal - le - lu - jah! Je - sus Christ shall ev - er reign!

reign! Hal - le - lu - jah, Hal - le - lu - jah! Je - sus Christ shall ev - er reign!

* The *ff* passages should be sung by the full Choir, the whole Congregation joining.
† Small notes for the instrument.

FINE.

1. Hear, O sin - ner! mer - cy hails you; Now with sweet - est voice she calls;
D. C.—Hear, O sin - ner! Hear, O sin - ner! 'Tis the voice of mer - cy calls.

Bids you haste to seek the Sav - iour, Ere the hand of just - ice falls:

Antiphonal Tune.

2 See the universe in motion,
    Sinking on her funeral pyre—
Earth dissolving, and the ocean
    Vanishing in final fire:—
      Hark, the trumpet!
Loud proclaims that Day of Ire!

3 Graves have yawn'd in countless numbers,
    From the dust the dead arise:
Millions, out of silent slumbers,
    Wake in undisturbed surprise;
      Where creation,
Wreck'd and torn in ruin lies!

4 See the Judge our nature wearing,
    Pure, ineffable, divine:—
See the great Archangel bearing
    High in heaven the mystic sign;
      Cross of Glory!
Christ be in that moment mine!

5 Every eye shall then behold him,
    Robed in awful majesty:—
Those that set at naught and sold him,
    Pierced and nailed him to a tree—
      Deeply wailing,
Shall the true Messiah see!

6 Lo! the last long separation!
    As the cleaving crowds divide;
And one dread adjudication
    Sends each soul to either side!
      Lord of mercy!
How shall I that day abide!

7 O, may thine own Bride and Spirit
    Then avert a dreadful doom—
And me summon to inherit
    An eternal blissful home:—
      Ah! come quickly!
Let thy second Advent come!

8 Yea, Amen! Let all adore thee,
    On thine amaranthine throne!
Saviour—take the power and glory,
    Claim the kingdom for thine own!
      Men and angels
Kneel and bow to thee alone!

Toledo.

2 See! the storm of vengeance gathering
    O'er the path you dare to tread!
Hark! the awful thunder rolling
    Loud and louder o'er your head!
      Turn, O sinner!
Lest the lightning strike you dead.

3 Haste, O sinner! to the Saviour;
    Seek his mercy while you may;
Soon the day of grace is over;—
    Soon your life must pass away;
      Haste, O sinner!
You must perish if you stay.

UTICA. 7s & 6s.

Z.

1. To thee, my God and Sa - vior! My heart ex - ult - ing sings, Re -

joic - ing in thy fa - vor, Al - migh - ty King of kings! I'll

cel - e-brate thy glo - ry, With all thy saints a - bove, And tell the joy - ful

sto - ry Of thy re-deem-ing love.

2 Soon as the morn with roses
  Bedecks the dewy east,
And when the sun reposes
  Upon the ocean's breast;
My voice, in supplication,
  Well-pleased the Lord shall hear;
Oh! grant me thy salvation,
  And to my soul draw near.

3 By thee, through life supported,
  I'll pass the dangerous road,
With heavenly hosts escorted,
  Up to thy bright abode;
Then cast my crown before thee,
  And all my conflicts o'er, .
Unceasingly adore thee;—
  What could an angel more?

1. Thou, O Lord, in ten - der love, Dost all my bur - dens bear;
2. Care - ful with - out care I am, Nor feel my hap - py toil;

Lift my heart to things a - bove, And fix it ev - er there.
Kept in peace by Je - sus' name, Sup - port - ed by His smile.

Calm on tu - mult's wheel I sit 'Midst bu - sy mul - ti - tudes a - lone;
Joy - ful thus my faith to show, I find His ser - vice my re - ward;

Sweet-ly wait - ing at Thy feet, Till all Thy will be done.
Eve - ry work I do be - low, I do it to the Lord.

3 To the desert or the cell,
  Let others blindly fly,
In this evil world I dwell,
  Unhurt, unspotted I.
Here I find a house of prayer,
  To which I inwardly retire;
Walking unconcerned in care,
  And unconsumed in fire.

COLUMBUS. 7s & 6s.

Z.

1. Hail to the Lord's a - noint - ed, Great Da-vid's great-er Son! Hail in the time ap - point - ed, His reign on earth be - gun! He comes to break op - pres - sion, To set the cap-tive free, To take a-way trans-gres - sion, And rule in e - qui - ty.

2 He comes with succor speedy,
　To those who suffer wrong;
To help the poor and needy,
　And bid the weak be strong;
To give them songs for sighing
　Their darkness turn to light,
Whose souls, condemned and dying,
　Were precious in his sight.

3 He shall come down like showers
　Upon the fruitful earth,
And love, and joy, like flowers,
　Spring in his path to birth:
Before him on the mountains,
　Shall Peace the herald go,
And righteousness, in fountains,
　From hill to valley flow.

Z.

1. Lamb of God! whose bleeding love We now re-call to mind, Send the an-swer from a-bove, And let us mer-cy find; Think on us who think of thee; Eve-ry bur-dened soul re-lease; Oh! re-mem-ber Cal-va-ry, And bid us go in peace.

2 Let thy blood, by faith applied,
  The sinner's pardon seal ;
Speak us freely justified,
  And all our sickness heal :
By thy passion on the tree,
  Let our griefs and troubles cease ;
Oh ! remember Calvary,
  And bid us go in peace.

3 Can we ever hence depart
  Till thou our wants relieve ?
Write forgiveness on our heart,
  And all thine image give :
Still our souls shall cry to thee
  Till renewed by holiness,—
Oh ! remember Calvary,
  And bid us go in peace.

MONADNOCK. 7s & 6s.

Z.

1. Now be the gospel - ban-ner To eve-ry land un-furled; And be the shout,—Ho-

san - na! Re-ech-oed through the world; Till eve-ry isle and na - tion, Till

eve-ry tribe and tongue Re-ceive the great sal - va - tion, And join the happy throng.

Monadnock.

1 Now be the gospel-banner
  In every land unfurled;
  And be the shout,—" Hosanna !"—
  Reechoed through the world;
  Till every isle and nation,
    Till every tribe and tongue
  Receive the great salvation,
    And join the happy throng.

2 What, though th' embattled legions
  Of earth and hell combine?
  His arm, throughout their regions,
  Shall soon resplendent shine :

Ride on, O Lord! victorious,
  Immanuel, Prince of peace !
Thy triumph shall be glorious,—
  Thy empire still increase.

3 Yes—thou shalt reign forever,
  O Jesus, King of kings !
Thy light, thy love, thy favor,
  Each ransomed captive sings:
The isles for thee are waiting,
  The deserts learn thy praise,
The hills and valleys greeting,
  The song responsive raise.

1. Meet and right it is to sing, In ev-ery time and place;
2. Thee, the first-born sons of light, In cho-ral sym-pho-nies,

Glo-ry to our heaven-ly King, The God of truth and grace.
Praise by day, day with-out night, And nev-er, nev-er cease;

Join we then with sweet ac-cord, All in one thanksgiv-ing join!
An-gels and arch-an-gels, all Praise the mys-tic Three in One;

Ho-ly, ho-ly, ho-ly Lord, E-ter-nal praise be thine!
Sing, and stop, and gaze, and fall, O'erwhelm'd be-fore Thy throne!

3 Father, God, Thy love we praise,
    Which gave Thy Son to die;
Jesus, full of truth and grace,
    Alike we glorify;
Spirit, Comforter divine,
    Praise by all to Thee be given,
Till we in full chorus join,
    And earth is turn'd to heaven.

ORLANDO. 7s & 6s.

CHORAL MOVEMENT.

Arranged from ORLANDO DI LASSO.

1. Re - deem - er! grant thy bless - ing! O! teach us how to pray, That

each, thy fear pos - sess - ing, May tread life's on - ward way: Then

where the pure are dwell - ing, We hope to meet a - gain; And

sweet - er num - bers swell - ing, For ev - er praise thy name.

Z.

1. To Je-sus, the crown of my hope, My soul is in haste to be gone; Oh!

bear me, ye cher-u-bim! up, And waft me a-way to his throne.

Page.

1 To Jesus, the crown of my hope,
   My soul is in haste to be gone;
   Oh! bear me, ye cherubim, up,
   And waft me away to his throne.

2 My Savior, whom absent I love,
   Whom not having seen, I adore;
   Whose name is exalted above
   All glory, dominion, and power;

3 Dissolve thou these bonds that detain
   My soul from her portion in thee;
   Oh! strike off this adamant chain,
   And make me eternally free.

4 When that happy era begins,
   When arrayed in thy glories I shine,

Nor grieve any more by my sins
The bosom on which I recline:

5 Oh, then shall the veil be removed,
   And round me thy brightness be pour'd;
   I shall see him whom absent I loved,
   Whom not having seen, I adored.

Another Hymn.

1 This God is the God we adore,
   Our faithful, unchangeable Friend;
   Whose love is as large as his power,
   And neither knows measure nor end.

2 'Tis Jesus, the First and the Last,
   Whose Spirit shall guide us safe home;
   We'll praise him for all that is past,
   And trust him for all that's to come

ALAUDA. 6s.

Z.

SOLO.

1. Flung to the heedless winds, Or to the wa-ters cast, Their ash-es shall be
2. Je - sus has now re - ceived Their lat - est liv - ing breath; Yet vain is Sa-tan's

Accomp.

watched, And gathered at the last; And 'from that scattered dust, A
boast Of vic-tory in their death; For still, tho' dead, they speak, And

round us and a - broad, Shall spring a plenteous seed Of wit-nesses for
loud from heav'n pro-claim, to many a wak'ning land, The one a-vail-ing

Chorus.

God. Shall spring a plenteous seed Of wit-ness - es for God, Shall

name, To many a wak'ning land The one a-vail - ing name, To

spring a plen-teous seed, Of wit-ness-es for God.

many a wak'-ning land, The one a-vail-ing name.

UNION.   6s & 4s.   z.

God bless our native land! | Firm may she ever stand; | Thro' storm and night; { When the wild
Ruler of

tempests rave. }
winds and wave, { Do thou our country save, | By thy great might, { By thy great might.

Union.

2 For her our prayer shall rise
   To God above the skies;
       On Him we wait;
   Thou who hast heard each sigh,
   Watching each weeping eye,
   Be Thou for ever nigh ;—
       . God save the State!

LYNN. 8s Double.

Z.

1. O Thou who hast spread out the skies, And measured the depths of the sea, Our

in - cense of praise shall a - rise, In joy - ous thanks-giv-ing to thee. For -

ev - er thy pres - ence is near, Tho' heaves our bark far from the land; We

ride on the deep with-out fear; The wa - ters are held in thy hand.

Melody of the Twelfth Century.

1. Fair - est Lord Je - sus! Ruler of all na - ture! O Thou of God and
1. Schön-ster Herr Je - su! Herrscher aller En - den! Got - - tes und Ma -

man the Son! Thee will I cher - ish, Thee will I hon - or, Thou!
ri - ä Sohn! Dich will ich lie - ben, Dich will ich eh - ren, Du

my soul's glo - ry, joy, and crown.
mein - er See - len Freud, und Kron!

2 Fair are the meadows,
   Fairer still the woodlands,
Robed in the blooming garb of spring,
   Jesus is fairer,
   Jesus is purer,
Who makes the woeful heart to sing.

3 Fair is the sunshine,
   Fairer still the moonlight,
And the twinkling starry host;
   Jesus shines brighter,
   Jesus shines purer,
Than all the angels heaven can boast.

Lynn.

1 O thou, who hast spread out the skies,
   And measured the depths of the sea,
Our incense of praise shall arise
   In joyous thanksgiving to thee.
Forever thy presence is near,
   Though heaves our bark far from the land;
We ride on the deep without fear;
   The waters are held in thy hand.

2 Eternity comes in the sound
   Of billows that never can sleep;
Jehovah encircles us round;
   Omnipotence walks on the deep.
Our Father, we look up to thee,
   As on tow'rd the haven we roll;
And faith in our Pilot shall be
   An anchor to steady the soul.

Crusaders' Hymn.

2 Schön sind die Felder,
   Noch schöner sind die Wälder,
In der schönen Frünlingszeit:
   Jesus ist schöner,
   Jesus ist reiner,
Der unser traurig Herz erfreut.

3 Schön leucht't die Sonne,
   Noch schöner leucht't der Monde,
Und die Sternlein allzumal;
   Jesus leucht't schöner,
   Jesus leucht't reiner,
Als all die Engel in Himmelssaal.

* This piece of music was first introduced in this country by R. Storrs Willis, Esq., by whose permission it is here inserted. It is deserving of a place in every collection of Psalmody. According to the traditionary text by which it is accompanied, it was wont to be sung by the German knights on their way to Jerusalem. The only hymn of the same century which, in point of style, resembles this, is one quoted in Burney from the Chatelaine de Coucy, set about the year 1190, very far inferior, however, to this. At a missionary meeting held lately in the principality of Lippe Detmold, this hymn was commenced by three voices, but ere the third verse was reached, hundreds joined in the heart-stirring song of praise.

BLUM. 10s.

Rise, crowned with light, im . pe - rial Sa-lem rise! | Ex - alt thy towering

head, and lift thine eyes! | See heaven, its sparkling por - tals

wide dis - play, | And break up - on thee in a flood of

day, | And break up - on thee in a flood of day.

WILLOW. 10s.

Go to the grave in all thy glorious prime, | In full ac - tiv - i - ty of zeal and power; | A Christian can - not die before his time; | The Lord's appointment is the servant's hour.

RESURGAM. 5s.

Slow.

Arranged by Z.

There's rest in the grave, | Life's toils are all past, | Night cometh at last:

1st Ending. 2d Ending.

{ How calm - ly I rest | In the sleep of the blest,
{ Nor hear life's storm rave | O'er my green grassy . . . grave.

* Sing thus the second time.

2. No rest in the grave—
Heaven's dawn purples fast,
Morn's splendors are cast
Like shafts through the gloom
Of the dark, silent tomb;
Heaven's fair bowers wave—
No rest in the grave!

3. Arise from the grave!
Heaven's bright, burning throng
Come rushing along;
They gird me about,
And triumphant shout,
As myriad palms wave,
"Ascend from the grave."

LUTHER. 10s.

B. WYMAN.

Al - might - y power! whose word and will sus - tain | Un -

- num - bered worlds, by some mys - te - rious chain; | Whose

links of air un - seen we know to be,

Firm as all love and truth that comes from thee.

Z.

1. The day is gone, the weary sun declining Behind the hills,—and now the stars are shining,— But Jesus, Sun of Righteousness, a-bide, Nor from my soul thy gracious presence hide.

2.

'Twere utter darkness here, if thou shouldst fail me,
Where all the pow'rs of evil would assail me,
And plunge me into deeps of endless night,
Without one star to shed its glimm'ring light.

3.

Accept, O God of grace, for daily favors,
Which now and ever prompt to good endeavors,
My offer'd thanks !—and may their incense rise,
By love's pure flame enkindled from the skies.

4.

Of every wrong this day I've done before thee,
Through thy dear Son, for pardon I implore thee;
And when in sleep I rest my weary head,
Be still thy wings of love around me spread!

5.

And when life's day by night shall be o'ertaken,
May then my soul, its faith in thee unshaken,
From death's dark vale with angels soar away
To where thy presence makes eternal day.

The spa - cious fir - ma - ment on high, With all the blue e - the - real sky, And

spangled heav'ns—a shining frame, Their great o - ri - gin - al proclaim. Th' unwearied

sun, from day to day, Doth his Cre - a - tor's power display; And pub - lish - es to

eve - ry land, The work of an Al - migh - ty hand, And pub - lish - es to eve - ry land the work of an Al-mighty hand, of an Al - migh-ty hand.

FARLEY. P. M.

1. Our blest Re - deem-er, ere he breathed His ten-der, last fare-well, A

2. He came in tongues of liv - ing flame, To teach, con - vince, sub - due; All

Guide, a Comforter be - queathed, With us to dwell, With us to dwell.

power-ful as the wind he came, As view-less too, As view - less too.

3 He came sweet influence to impart,
    A gracious, willing guest ;
While he can find one humble heart,
    Wherein to rest.

4 And his that gentle voice we hear,
    Soft as the breath of even;
That checks each fault, that calms each fear,
    And speaks of heaven.

5 And every virtue we possess,
    And every victory won,
And every thought of holiness,
    Are his alone.

6 Spirit of purity and grace,
    Our weakness pitying see :
O make our hearts thy dwelling-place,
    And worthier thee.

* Small notes for the first, large notes for the following verses.

CHANTING STYLE.
Bass or Alto Solo, or Chorus from the Organ Score.

Z.

1. What sin-ners val-ue   I resign: Lord!'tis enough that thou art mine: I shall behold thy

Organ.

Ped.

Bass Chorus. *pp*

blissful face, And stand complete in   righ-teous-ness. This life's a dream, an empty show,

p

Swell.

Ped.

Bass & Tenor.   Solo.

f

But the bright world to which I go Hath joys substantial and sincere; When shall I wake and

Great Op. & St.
Organ.   Diap.

Swell.

Ped.

find me there?   Chorus—Allegro.

O, glo-rious hour! O, blest a-bode! I shall be

ff

Echo, *with Dulcima.*
or, *if there be none, with Diap.*

ff

near and like my God! And flesh and sin no more con - trol The sa - cred

plea-sures of the soul, The sa - cred plea-sures of the soul. My flesh shall slumber

in the ground, Till the last trumpet's joyful sound; Then burst the chains with sweet sur - prise, And

in my Sa - vior's im - age rise, And in my Sa - vior's im - age rise.

Bassi p

Organ.

Tenor.

f

f

Ped.

* Trumpet

ALLEGRO MODERATO.

Praise, Ju-dah, praise thy King! To thee the Ho - ly came; Yet shall thy voice his

Praise, Ju - dah, praise thy King! To thee the Ho - ly came; Yet shall thy voice his

good-ness sing, Thy faith shall own his name; Yet shalt thou bless that cross, Thine

good-ness sing, Thy faith shall own his name; Yet shalt thou bless that cross, Thine

own re - jec - tion gave, And own all o - ther wealth but dross, For

own re - jec - tion gave, And own all o - ther wealth but dross, For him who died to save.   In

Alto or Bass.

him who died to save.   Ye Gen - tiles, lift your voice! In

Organ.

dark - ness long ye lay; Now in the light of truth re - joice, And

dark - ness long ye lay; Now in the light of truth re - joice, And

Solo.

praise to Je - sus pay, Now in the light of truth re - joice, And

praise to Je - sus pay, Now in the light of truth re - joice, And praise to Je - sus pay. Ye is - lands of the

praise to Je - sus pay. Alto or Bass. Ye is - lands of the seas! Ye is - lands of the

seas! Ye na - tions of the West! Swell

seas! Ye na - tions of the West! Ye na - tions of the West!

forth your songs on eve - ry breeze, Swell forth your songs on eve - ry breeze, To

Swell forth your songs on eve - ry breeze, on eve - - ry breeze, To

Swell forth your songs on eve - ry breeze, To

Swell forth your songs on eve - ry breeze, on eve - ry breeze, To speak your Sa - vior blest, To speak your Sa - vior blest, To speak your

speak your Sa - vior blest, To speak your Sa - vior blest, To speak your Sa - vior

speak your Sa - vior blest, To speak your Sa - vior blest, To speak your

Sa - vior blest, To speak your Sa - vior blest! Swell forth your

blest, To speak your Sa - vior blest! Swell forth your songs on

Sa - vior blest, To speak your Sa - vior blest! Swell forth your

songs, To speak your Sa-vior blest! Swell forth your songs To

eve-ry breeze, To speak your Sa-vior blest! Swell forth your songs to eve-ry breeze, To

songs, To speak your Sa-vior blest! Swell forth your songs To speak your Sa - vior blest!

speak your Sa - vior blest!

Organ *ff*

speak your Sa - vior blest!   Pedal.

p   *p*

Thou, heaven, in rap - turous shout, The ju - bi - lee pro -

p   *p*

Thou, heaven, in rap - turous shout, The ju - bi - lee pro -

p

f   *p*

long! Ye chim-ing spheres, a - gain ring out Your u - ni - ver - sal song! Ye

f   *p*

long! Ye chim-ing spheres, a - gain ring out Your u - ni - ver - sal song! Ye

f   *p*

f   *p*

an - gels who re - joice   A - bove one res-cued   soul,   Now from each glowing

an - gels who re - joice   A - bove one res-cued   soul,   Now from each glowing

se-raph's voice Let   strains   of   tri - umph   roll !   Let   strains   of   tri-umph

se-raph's voice Let   strains   of   tri - umph   roll !   Let   strains   of

Let   strains   of   tri-umph

roll !   Let   strains   of   tri - umph   roll !   Let   strains   of   tri - umph

tri-umph roll !   Let   strains   of   tri-umph roll !   Let   strains   of

roll !   Let   strains   of   tri - umph   roll !   Let   strains   of   tri - umph

roll! Let strains of tri - umph roll! Let strains of tri - umph
tri-umph roll! Let strains of tri - umph roll! Let strains of
roll! Let strains of tri - umph roll! Let strains of tri - umph
Maestoso.
ff
roll! Let strains of tri-umph roll! Let
tri-umph roll! Let strains of tri-umph roll! Let
Organ.
p
Maestoso.
roll! Let strains of tri-umph roll! Let
strains of tri - umph roll!
strains of tri - umph roll!
Ped.
strains of tri - umph roll!

For third verse.

1 Wilt Thou not visit me?
The plant beside me feels Thy gentle dew;
  Each blade of grass I see,
From Thy deep earth its quick'ning moisture
    drew.

2 Wilt Thou not visit me?
Thy morning calls on me with cheering tone;
  And every hill and tree
Lend but one voice, the voice of Thee alone.

3 Come! for I need thy love,
More than the flower the dew, or grass the rain;
  Come, like Thy holy dove,
And let me in Thy sight rejoice to live again.

4 Yes! Thou wilt visit me;
Nor plant, nor tree, Thine eye delights so well,
  As when from sin set free,
Man's spirit comes with Thine in peace to dwell

PSALM 100.

1. O, be joyful in the Lord, ... all | ye | lands;
3. O, go your way into his gates with thanksgiving, and into his | courts | with | praise;
5. Now unto the .... King | e- | ternal,

2. Be ye sure that the Lord .... he | is | God;
4. For the Lord is gracious, his mercy is .... ev - | er- | lasting;
6. Be honor and glory through .... Je - | sus | Christ,

PSALM 103.

1. Praise the Lord, ... O | my | soul,
2. Praise the Lord, ... O | my | soul,
3. Who forgiveth .... all | thy | sin,
4. Who saveth thy .... life | from de- | struction;
5. O, praise the Lord, ye angels of his, ye that ex- .... cel | in | strength,
6. O, praise the Lord, all .... ye, | his | hosts,
7. O, speak good of the Lord, all ye works of his, in all places of | his | do- | minion;
8. Now unto the .... King | e- | ternal,
9. Be honor and glory through .... Je - | sus | Christ,

DOUBLE CHANT.

serve the Lord with gladness, and come before his .. | pres - ence | with a | song. 2.
be thankful unto him, and .... | speak good | of his | name. 4.
immortal, invisible, the .... | ou - ly | wise.... | God; 6.

it is he that hath made us, and not we ourselves; we are his | people, and the | sheep of his | pasture. 3.
and his truth endureth from gene- .... | ration to | gen - e- | ration. 5.
forever and .... | ev - er. | A..... | men.

PSALM 103.　　z

and all that is within me .... | praise his | ho - ly | name.
and for-.. | get not | all his | benefits.
and .... | heal - eth | all thine in- | firmities.
and crowneth thee with .... | mercy and | lov - ing | kindness.
ye that fulfill his commandment, and hearken unto the | voice of | his...... | word.
ye servants of .... | his, that | do his | pleasure.
praise thou the............................... | Lord,..... | O my | soul.
immortal, invisible, the........................ | on - ly | wise..... | God;
forever and.................................... | ev - er. | A...... | men.

DOUBLE CHANT.

SELECTION No. 1.

SOLI.

Psalm cxxi.

1. I will lift up mine eyes unto the hills from hence	cometh my	help.
3. He will not suffer thy foot to be moved: He that keepeth thee	will not	slumber.
5. The Lord is thy keeper, the Lord is thy shade upon thy ...	right	hand.
7. The Lord shall preserve thee from all evil; He shall pre -	serve thy	soul.

Psalm xlvii.

1. O, clap your hands, all ye people: shout unto God with the	voice of	triumph.
3. He shall subdue the people under us, and the nations	under our	feet.
5. God is gone up with a shout, the Lord with the	sound of a	trumpet.
7. For God is the King of all the earth; sing ye praises	with under-	standing.
9. The princes of the people are gathered together, even the people of the	God of	Abraham.

Psalm xxx.

1. I will extol thee, O Lord; for thou hast lifted me up, and hast not made my foes to re - - - - - - - - - -	joice over	me.
3. O Lord, thou hast brought up my soul from the grave: thou hast kept me alive, that I should not go	down to the	pit.
5. For his anger endureth but a moment; in his favor is life: weeping may endure for a night, but joy cometh.........	in the	morning.
7 Lord, by thy favor thou hast made my mountain to stand strong: thou didst hide thy face, and	I was	troubled.
9. What profit is there in my blood, when I go down to the pit? Shall the dust praise thee? shall it de - - - -	clare thy	truth?
11. Thou hast turned for me my mourning into dancing: thou hast put off my sackcloth and	girded me with	gladness;

CHORUS.

13. O Lord, my God, O Lord, my God, I will give thanks un - to

J. Z.

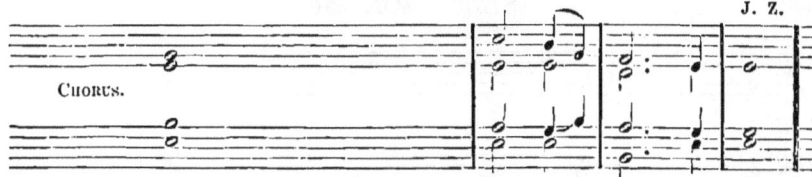

CHORUS.

Psalm cxxi.

2. My help cometh from the Lord	which made	heaven and	and earth.
4. Behold, he that keepeth Israel..............	shall not	slumber nor	sleep.
6. The sun shall not smite thee by day,.........	nor tho	moon by	night.
8. The Lord shall preserve thy going out and thy coming in, from this time forth, and	even for	ev - er -	more.*

Psalm xlvii.

2. For the Lord most high is terrible; he is a great	king over	all tho	earth.
4. He shall choose our inheritance for us, the excellency of..............................	Ja - cob,	whom he	loved.
6. Sing praises to God, sing praises, sing praises unto our....	King, sing	prai - -	ses.
8. God reigneth over the heathen: God sitteth upon the	throne of his	ho - li -	ness.
10. For the shields of the earth belong unto God: he is................................	great - ly ex-	- alt - -	ed.*

Psalm xxx.

2. O Lord, my God, I cried unto thee, and	thou hast...	heal - ed	me.
4. Sing unto the Lord, O ye Saints of his, and give thanks at the remembrance	of his	ho - li -	ness.
6. And in my prosperity, I said, I shall	nev - er be	mov - -	ed.
8. I cried to thee, O Lord; and unto the Lord I..	made suppli-	- ca - -	tion.
10. Hear, O Lord, and have mercy upon me: Lord, be.................................	thou my	help - -	er.
12. To the end that my glory may sing praise to thee, and	not be	si - - -	lent.

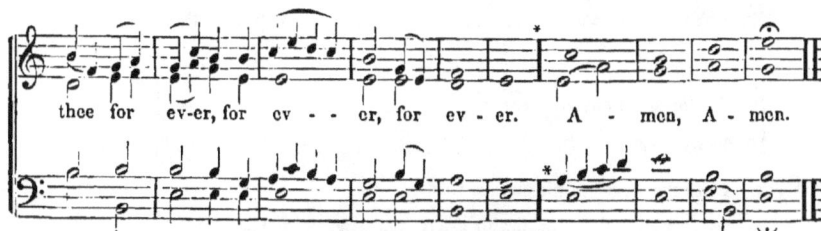

thee for   ev-er, for   ev - - er, for   ev - er.   A - men, A - men.

* "Amen" to be sung after each Psalm.

Psalm ciii.

1. Bless the Lord........	O	my	soul;
3. Who forgiveth all thine in - - - - - - - -	i	qui -	ties;
5. Who satifieth thy mouth with..................	good - - -		things;
7. He made known his ways.....................	un - to		Moses, '
9 He will not.................................	al - ways		chide;
11. For as the heaven is high a - - - - - -	bove	the	earth,
13. Like as a father.............................	pitieth	his	children,
15. As for man, his.............................	days are as		grass;
17. But the mercy of the Lord is from everlasting to everlasting upon.........................	them	that	fear him;
19. The Lord has prepared his....................	throne in the		heavens;
21. Bless ye the Lord, all.......................	ye	his	hosts;

2. Bless the Lord,.............................	O	my	soul
4. Who redeemeth thy life......................	from	de -	struction;
6. The Lord executeth righteousness and	judg - - -		ment
8. The Lord is merciful and......................	gra - - - -		cious,
10. He has not dealt with us.........	after	our	sins;
12. As far as the east is...........................	from	the	west,
14. For he...............................	knoweth our		frame;
16. For the wind passeth over it....................	and it	is	gone;
18. To such as................................	keep	his	convenant,
20. Bless the Lord, ye his angels, that ex - - - -	cel	in	strength,
22. Bless the Lord, all his works in all places of.....	his	do -	minion:

Psalm ciii.

and all that is within me	bless his	ho - ly	name.	2
who	heal - eth	all thy dis-	eases;	4
so that thy youth is re - - - - -	new - ed	like the	eagle's.	6
his acts unto the	chil - dren	of	Israel.	8
neither will he	keep his	anger for	ever.	10
so great is his mercy toward.........	them that	fear	him.	12
so the Lord pitieth.............	them that	fear	him.	14
as a flower of the..............	field - - -	so he	flourisheth.	16
and his righteousness un - - - - -	to the	chil - dren's	children;	18
and his kingdom........... ...	rul - eth	ov - er	all.	20
ye ministers of...............	his, that	do his	pleasure.	22

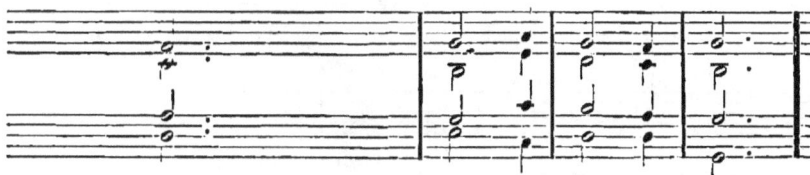

and for - - - - - - - - - - -	get not	all his	benefits.	3
who crowneth thee with loving........	kindness and	ten - der	mercies.	5
for................................	all that	are op-	pressed.	7
slow to anger, and.................	plen - - -	teous in	mercy.	9
nor rewarded us ac - - - - - -	cording to	our in -	iquities.	11
so far has he removed..............	our trans -	gressions from	us.	13
he remembers that.................	we	are	dust.	15
and the place thereof shall..........	know it	no	more.	17
and to those that remember his com -	mandments	to do	them.	19
that do his commandments, hearkening unto the	voice.....	of his	word.	21
Bless the Lord,...................	O.......	my	soul.	

Allegro Moderato.

f

Glo-ry be to God on high; And on earth peace, good will towards men. We praise thee, we bless } thee, we {

Glo-ry be to God on high; And on earth peace, good will towards men. We praise thee, we bless } thee, we {

ff

worship thee, we glorify thee, we give thanks to thee for } thy great glory; O Lord God, heavenly

worship thee, we glorify thee, we give thanks to thee for } thy great glo-ry; O Lord God, heavenly

SOPRANO SOLO.

King, God the Father Al-migh-ty. O... Lord, the only begotten Son, Jes-us

Slower.

f ORGAN, *colla parte.*

King, God the Father Al-migh-ty.

TENOR SOLO. *Lento.*

Christ; O Lord God, Lamb of God, Son of the Father, } sins of the world.
that takest away the {

SOPRANO AND ALTO.

Have mer-cy up-on us.

Basso Solo.
Tenor.
Basso.
Tenor.
Thou that takest away the sins of the world, have mer-cy up-on us.
Thou that takest away the sins of the world, re-ceive our prayer.
Alto.
Alto.
Have mer-cy up-on us.
Re-ceive our prayer.
Basso Solo.
Tenor. ritard.
Thou that sittest at the right hand of God the Father,
Have mer-cy up-on us.
Alto.
Have mer-cy up-on us.
f Allegro Moderato.
For thou on-ly art ho-ly, Thou on-ly art the Lord, Thou on-ly, O Christ, with the
For thou on-ly art ho-ly, Thou on-ly art the Lord, Thou on-ly, O Christ, with the
Slower.
Ho-ly Ghost, art most high in the glo-ry of God...... the Fa-ther. A-men.
Ho-ly Ghost, Art most high in the glo-ry of God.......... the Fa-her. A-men.

1. Glory be   to | God   on | high,
2. We praise Thee, we bless Thee, we | wor - ship | Thee,

and on earth, | peace, good | will towards | men.
we glorify Thee, we give thanks to | Thee for | Thy great | glory.

3. O Lord God | heaven - ly | King;
4. O Lord, the only begotten Son | Je - sus | Christ;

God the | Fa - ther | all - | mighty.
O Lord God, Lamb of | God, Son | of the | Father.

SOLI.

5. That takest away   the | sins of the | world, | Have mercy | up - | on us.
6. Thou that takest away the | sins of the | world, | Have mercy | up - | on us.
7. Thou that takest away the | sins of the | world, | Re - | ceive our | prayer.

8. Thou that sittest at the right hand of | God the | Father, |

Have | mercy up - | on | us. | 9. For thou | only art | holy, |

Thou | on - ly | art the | Lord. | 10. Thou only, O Christ, with the |

Ho - ly | Ghost, | art most high in the | Glory of |

God the | Father. | A - | men. | A - - - | men.

* May be omited.

CHANT ANTHEM. Ps. XV.

John Zundel

TENOR.
Lord, who shall abide in thy Ta-ber-na-cle? Who shall dwell in thy ho - ly hill?

Organ.

BASS.
He that walketh uprightly, and worketh righteousness, and speaketh the truth in his

ALTO.
heart. He that backbiteth not with his tongue, nor doeth e-vil to his neighbor,

TENOR.
nor taketh up a re-proach against his neighbor. In whose eyes a vile person is con-

temn-ed ; but he honoreth them that fear the Lord. He that sweareth to his own

hurt, and changeth not. He that putteth not out his money to usury, nor taketh reward a-

gainst the in - no - cent. He that do - eth these things,

He that doeth these things, shall nev - er be mov-ed,

shall nev - er, shall nev - er be mov - - - ed.

CONGREGATION.

He that do-eth these things,   He that do-eth these things, shall nev - er, shall

AIR.

He that do-eth these things,   He that do-eth these things, shall nev - er, shall

nev - er, shall nev - er be mov - ed, shall nev - er be mov - ed.

nev - er, shall nev - er be mov - ed, shall nev - er be mov - ed.

GOLDEN SHORE.   J. ZUNDEL.

CHOIR. TREBLE & ALTO.

1. Lo! the seal of death is break-ing; Those who slept its sleep are

Instrument.

waking; Hea - ven opes its por - tals fair! Hea - ven opes its por-tals fair!

CONGREGATION.

Hark! the harps of God are ring - ing, Hark! the se - raph's hymn is

AIR.

Hark! the harps of God are ring - ing, Hark! the se - raph's hymn is

fling - ing Mu - sic on im - mortal air, Mu - sic on im - mor-tal air.

fling - ing Mu - sic on im - mortal air, Mu - sic on im - mor-tal air.

2 There, no more at eve declining,
  Suns without a cloud are shining
    O'er the land of life and love;
  There the founts of life are flowing,
  Flowers unknown to time, are blowing,
    In that radiant scene above.

4 There no sigh of memory swelleth,
  There no tear of misery welleth;
    Hearts will bleed or break no more;
  Past is all the cold world's scorning,
  Gone the night, and broke the morning,
    Over all the golden shore.

GOD OUR REFUGE.

Arr. from Dr. MARTIN LUTHER'S CHORAL, by J. Z.

1. God is our ref - uge and de - fence; | Our shield his dread om-
2. There is a riv - er calm and pure | Where streams refresh and
3. God is our ref - uge and our shield: | What then can make us

nipotence: Earth may be - neath us shrink; | The
well secure The dwell - ing - place of God; | Blest
fear or yield? Wars at his bid - ding cease; | He

an - cient moun - tains hoar Down in the
ci - ty, fair and bright, His fa - vor'd
breaks the bow and spear, He reigns in

deep tide sink; Let the wild del - uge roar! | Jehovah is our
saint's a - bode, Where the Lord reigns in light; | No foe can shake his
truth and peace; Let all a - dore and fear | Our God and Saviour

ref - uge and de - fence!
strong found - a - tion sure.
Is - rael's help and shield. A - men. A - men.

Moderato.

E. MOORE.

How a - mia-ble, How a - mia-ble are thy ta-ber-na-cles, O Lord of Hosts.

rit.

How a - mia-ble, how a - mia-ble are thy tab-er-na-cles, O Lord of Hosts.

Earnestly.

Instr.

My soul longeth, yea, even faint-eth for the courts of the Lord,

And my heart and my

Allegro.

f Blessed are they that dwell in thy

flesh crieth out for the liv - ing God.

house, Blessed are they that dwell in thy house, They will be still praising thee, They will be

ff

Cres.

f3

still prais-ing thee. Hal-le - lu - jah, Hal-le - lu - jah, Hal-le - lu - jah, A - men.

Christmas Anthem.

Andante cantubile.

John Zundel

p f.

1. No war nor bat - tle's sound, Was heard the world around, No hostile chiefs to furious

3. And music, sweet and clear, Flowed on the listen - ing ear, Such as of old the sons of
5. O, may the sil - ver chime Sound thro' all com - ing time, And let the bass of heaven's deep

com - bat ran; But peaceful was the night, In which the Prince of light, His

morn - ing sung: The gen - tle Cher - u - bim, And shin - ing Ser - a - phim, Wel-
or - gan blow, To bless the Ho - ly Child, Who came in win - ter wild, To

reign of peace up - on the earth be - gan, His reign of peace up - on the

- comed their Prince, with rapt - ure on their tongue, Welcomed their Prince with rapture
dwell with man in this cold world be - low, To dwell with man in this cold

SOLO.

earth.... be - gan.   2. The shepherds on the lawn, Before the

on... .... their tongue. *Sym. pp*
world..... be - low.

CHORUS. *Allegro. ff*

break of dawn, Sat sil-ent, gaz-ing on the starry sky; When, lo! a blaze of

light Burst on their wondering sight, With fiery radiance kind - ling all on

high; With fiery radiance kindling all on high. *Sym. f*

* The Organ may repeat the four preceding measures *ff*, and suddenly drop to *p* after. No symphony between 3d and 4th verses.

Choir. *Soprano and Alto Solo.*

1. Christian, the morn breaks sweetly o'er thee, And all the midnight sha-dows flee,

INST.

Tinged are the dis - tant skies with glo - ry, A bea - con light hung out for thee.

CONGREGATION AND CHOIR.

Arise, arise ! the light breaks o'er thee, Thy name is graven on the throne ; Thy home is in the

world of glory, Where thy Redeemer reigns alone, Where thy Redeemer reigns alone.

Female Voices.

2. Tossed on time's rude, relentless surges, Calmly, composed and dauntless stand, For

* Play upper notes an octave higher.

lo ! be-yond those scenes e - merges   The light that bounds the promised land.

_f_ CONGREGATION.

Behold! behold! the land is nearing, Where the wild seastorm's rage is o'er ; Hark ! how the heav'nly

hosts are cheering, See in what throngs they range the shore ! See in what throngs they range the shore!

f Male Voices.   _dolce._

3. Cheer up ! cheer up ! the day breaks o'er thee, Bright as the summer's noontide ray ; The

star-gemm'd crowns and realms of glory In - vite thy hap - py soul a - way.

Chorus.

A-way, away! leave all for glory, Thy name is graven on the throne, Thy home is in that

world of glory, Where the Redeemer reigns alone, Where the Redeemer reigns alone.

SOLO AND CHANT. "Thy Will be done." J. Z.

Soli.

Chorus.

1. Thy will be done! Thy will be done! { In devious ways the nurrying stream of.....................
2. Thy will be done! Thy will be done! { If o'er us shine a gladd'ning and a.....................
3. Thy will be done! Thy will be done! { Tho' shrouded o'er our path with gloom, one comfort......

Organ.

life may run; { Yet still our grate- ful heart shall.... } say, Thy will be done, be done.
pros - p'rous sun, { This prayer will make it more di - } vine, Thy will be done, be done.
one is ours, { To breathe while we a - - - - } dore, Thy will be done, be done.

* Soprano, Solo, or Chorus ƒƒ.

Patriotic Chorus.

J. ZUNDEL.

Tempo di Marcia.

ff

TREBLE. *f*

ALTO.

1. Freedom's sons! come, join in cho-rus, Praise this fav - ored spot of
3. Freedom's sons! of ev - ery na - tion, Here a heart - y wel - come

TENOR.

BASS.

Fine

* May be sung as a Duett, by two female or two male voices ; or as a Terzett by omitting the Tenor.

earth ;   Praise the skies   now smil-ing o'er us, Praise the land which gave us
greet,   While no haugh - ty ty-rant frowning, E'er in-vades your calm re -

birth !   Tho' our sky is   oft - en frowning, Tho' our land is rough and
- treat.   Come, and help us   swell the cho - rus, Praise this hallowed spot of

scar ;   Health and peace our   la - bors crowning, Bless the cheerful spir - its
earth ;   Praise the skies now   smil-ing o'er us, Praise the land which gave us

here I
birth,

2. Here are e - qual rights de - fend-ed, Rich-es fill the bu - sy
4. Freedom's sons, throughout cre - a - tion, Shout the an - them loud and

hands ;   Then be   wel - come kind ex - tend - ed   To th'oppress'd from o - ther
clear,   Till the   op - pressed in   ev - ery nation Shall the joy - ful ti - dings

lands!   Let them come, and join the cho - rus Let them praise this spot   of
hear.   Then shall come, loud ring-ing o'er   us From all   na - tions, songs of

earth ; Praise the skies now smiling o'er us, Praise the land which gave us birth !
mirth,   Ech - oes of   one   mighty chorus From the whole en - franchised earth.

Allegro.
DUETTO OR TERZETTO.

1. O God of the Na - tions! our Coun - try we sing!— A
2. Fair land of the riv - er, the prai - rie, the lake, What

fond heart's de - vo - tion the trib - ute we bring— All
is there we would not re - sign for thy sake? Come

tri - al we wel - come, all dan - ger we dare For the home that we
peace or come pe - ril, O home of our pride! We'll live or we'll

ff CHORUS.

love and the ban - ner we bear. Flag of our Fa - thers! thy
die as the brav - est have died.

ff

stars shall not wane, Glo - ry at - tend thee on o - cean and

* Small notes to be played—or they may be sung, at pleasure.

shore, Float o'er the Free from the Gulf to the main—

God shall de - fend thee till states are no more! Float o'er the

Free from the Gulf to the main— God shall de -

After last verse.

- fend thee till states are no more. No more! No more!

3

We hail thee, we crown thee, bright land of the West!
God keep thee the purest, the noblest, the best,
Till all thy domain with a people He fills
As free as thy winds and as firm as thy hills.
    Chorus:—Flag of our Fathers! &c.

4

For honor, for virtue, for freedom, for God,
We'll follow the path that our fathers have trod,
Right onward, unswerving, till joyful we raise
From ocean to ocean an anthem of praise!
    Chorus:—Flag of our Fathers!—   Miss Edna Dean.

WAR HYMN.

Words by THEODORE TILTON. $\quad \bullet = 20$ Music by JOHN ZUNDEL.

1. Thou who ordain - est, for the land's sal - va - tion, Famine, and fire, and

2. By the great sign, foretold of Thy ap - pearing, Coming in clouds, while

sword, and la - men - ta - tion, Now unto Thee we lift our sup - pli - ca - tion, —

mortal men stand fear - ing, Show us, a - mid this smoke of bat - tle, clearing,

ritard.   *a tempo.*

Now un - to Thee we lift our sup - pli - ca - tion, God save the

Show us, a - mid this smoke of bat - tle, clear - ing, Thy char - iot

na - tion! God save the na - tion! God save the na - tion! God save the na - tion!

nearing! Thy chariot nearing! Thy chariot nearing! Thy char - iot nearing!

3.
By the brave blood that floweth like a river,
Hurl Thou a thunderbolt from out Thy quiver!
Break Thou the strong gates! Every fetter shiver!
  Smite and deliver!

4.
Slay Thou our foes, or turn them to derision, —
Till, through the blood-red Valley of Decision,
Peace on our fields shine, like a prophet's vision,
  Green and elysian!

Glo-ry be to the Father, and to the Son, and to the Ho - - - ly Ghost,

As it was in the beginning, is now, and ever shall be, world with - out end. A - men.

NOTE. 1st, 2d, 5th and 6th measures in chanting style, and strictly in time—3d, 4th and 7th to be sung "cantabile." The small notes are intended for the Organ accompaniment. The "cantabile" measures to be played as sung.

GLORIA TIBI.

z.

Glo - ry! Glo - ry! Glo-ry be to thee, O Lord, O Lord!

AMEN.

z.

A - men, A - men, A - - - men.

A - men, A - men, A - men, A - men, A - men, A - - - - - men.

ALPHABETICAL INDEX OF TUNES.

Tune	Page	Time*	Tune	Page	Time*
Abo	40	50	Herman	14	—
Alauda	108	77	Holliston	38	30
Ansonia	35	40	Hope	81	—
Anthony	83	36	Hosanna	5	35
Antiphonal Tune	98	60	Howitt	62	40
Arago	57	45			
Ararat	17	45	Ilsley	71	30
Astoria	47	30	Indianapolis	73	28
Bainbridge	33	38	Kidron	66	50
Bartholdy	75	40			
Beecher	91	65	Lafon	74	40
Benefactor	6	40	Landor	15	43
Bethel	85	36	Last Judgment	52	48
Bethlehem	16	60	Lebanon	55	—
Bladenburgh	18	35	Lexington	65	54
Blum	112	43	Life's Billows	86	58
Brand	95	45	Lincoln	27	32
Brooklyn	60	45	Louisville	48	26
			Luther	114	42
Calvary	19	26	Lynn	110	45
Carmel	58	44			
Choral	89	—	Mary	68	50
Christ Saving the Nation	25	55	Magdalene	70	45
Cincinnati	50	40	Milwaukee	87	40
Clara	18	38	Missouri	9	30
Columbus	102	40	Monadnock	104	45
Corinth	97	45	Morning	56	45
Cromwell	63	40	Mount Vernon	20	30
Crusaders' Hymn	111	48	Mount Zion	80	62
Crystal	49	28			
Cypress	21	40	Nashua	29	55
			Neander	28	55
Daybreak	14	40	Newark	74	30
Detroit	59	45	Newell	48	36
Devotion	88	65	Newtown	10	30
			New Haven	90	70
Eden	39	30	Niagara	51	25
Edith	69	45	Nightingale	32	35
Egelston	115	40			
Emilie	53	50	Oberlin	72	60
Esther	82	60	Oriole	61	38
Evening Devotion	34	55	Orion	12	55
			Orlando	106	75
Farley	117	33			
Fischer	36	50	Pacific	24	70
Freeport	7	50	Page	107	25
Frost	79	70	Paradise	26	58
			Peabody	41	55
Golden Shore	140	73	Pilgrim	93	70
			Pollock	103	50
Hartford	42	45	Promise	13	—
Harvard	77	50	Providence	44	25

* The time given is the number of seconds required for singing one verse.

	Page	Time
Raymond	64	48
Refuge	43	32
Resurgam	113	—
Ropes	6	45
Rose	30	30
Sampson	37	40
Sarah	20	32
Simpson	101	55
Sonora	44	30
Spring	46	45
Springfield	94	58
Star of Bethlehem	8	63
St. Petersburg	11	55
Stuttgart	84	60
Supplication	22	55
Syracuse	92	62
The Spacious Firmament	116	—
Toledo	99	—
Trenton	30	35
Twilight	67	—
Tyng	105	50
Union	109	40
Utica	100	45
Vasar	31	30
Victor	10	30
Vinton	78	47
Viola	38	30
Watchman	76	58
Watts	23	40
Welcome	96	42
Wesley	54	45

	Page	Time
Willow	113	35
Wilt thou not visit me	127	—
Yale	45	42

ANTHEMS.

	Page
Christian, the morn breaks sweetly o'er thee	147
Gloria in Excelsis, No. 1	134
Golden Shore	140
How amiable are Thy tabernacles	143
Lord, who shall abide	138
No war nor battle's sound (Christmas Anthem)	144
Praise, Judah, praise thy King	120
The spacious firmament	116
What sinners value I resign	118

CHANTS.

	Page
Amen	157
Bless the Lord, O my soul	132
Gloria in Excelsis, No. 2	136
Gloria Tibi	157
Gloria Patri	157
I will lift up mine eyes	130
I will extol Thee	130
O be joyful	128
O clap your hands	130
Praise the Lord, O my soul	123
Thy will be done	149

FOR SOCIABLE MEETINGS.

	Page
National Hymn : O God of the Nations	154
Patriotic Chorus : Freedom's Sons	150
War Hymn : Thou who ordainest	156

METRICAL INDEX.

L. M.

	Page
Ararat	17
Benefactor	6
Bethlehem (Double)	16
Bladenburgh	18
Calvary	19
Christ saving the Nation (6 Lines)	25
Clara	18
Cypress	21
Daybreak	14
Freeport	7
Herman	14
Hosanna	5
Landor	15
Lincoln	27
Missouri	9
Mount Vernon	20
Nashua (6 Lines)	29
Neander " "	28
Newtown	10
Orion (Double)	12
Pacific "	24
Paradise "	26
Promise	13

	Page
Ropes	6
Sarah	20
Star of Bethlehem (Double)	8
St. Petersburg (6 Lines)	11
Supplication (Double)	22
Victor	10
Watts	23

C. M.

	Page
Abo (Double)	40
Ansonia	35
Bainbridge	33
Eden	39
Evening Devotion (Double)	34
Fischer "	36
Hartford "	42
Holliston	38
Nightingale (12 Lines)	32
Peabody (Double)	41
Rose	30
Sampson	37
Trenton	30
Vasar	31
Viola	33

S. M.

	Page
Astoria	47
Cincinnati (Double)	50
Crystal	49
Emilie	53
Last Judgment (Double)	52
Lebanon "	55
Louisville	48
Newell	48
Niagara	51
Providence	44
Refuge	43
Sonora	44
Spring (Double)	46
Wesley "	54
Yale "	45

L. P. M. (II. 1.)

Morning	56

C. P. M. (II. 2.)

Arago	57
Carmel	58
Detroit	59

L. M. 6 Lines (II. 3).

Christ saving the Nation	25
Nashua	29
Neander	28
St. Petersburg	11

H. M. (II. 4.)

Brooklyn	60
Cromwell	63
Howitt	62
Oriole	61

7s. (III. 1.)

Bartholdy	75
Bethel	85
Edith	69
Esther (Double)	82
Harvard "	77
Indianapolis	73
Ilsley	71
Kidron (Double)	66
Lafon	74
Lexington (Double)	65
Mary "	68
Magdalene "	70
Newark	74
Oberlin (Double)	72
Raymond "	64
Twilight	67
Vinton	78
Watchman (Double)	76

7s. 6 Lines (III. 2).

	Page
Twilight	67

8s & 7s. (III. 3.)

Anthony	83
Beecher (Double)	91
Choral	89
Devotion (Double)	88
Esther "	82
Frost (Double)	79
Hope "	81
Life's Billows (Double)	86
Milwaukee	87
Mount Zion (Double)	80
New Haven "	90
Pilgrim "	93
Springfield (6 Lines)	94
Stuttgart (Double)	84
Syracuse "	92

8s, 7s, & 4s. (III. 5.)

Antiphonal Tune	98
Brand	95
Corinth	97
Toledo	99
Welcome	96

7s & 6s. (II. 6.)

Columbus	102
Monadnock	104
Orlando	106
Pollock	103
Simpson	101
Tyng	105
Utica	100

10s. (II. 5.)

Blum	112
Luther	114
Willow	113

10s & 11s. (IV. 1.)

Egelston	115

8s. (IV. 2.)

Alauda (Double)	108
Lynn "	110
Page	107

6s & 4s.

Union	109

5s, 6s, & 8s.

Crusaders' Hymn	111

5s.

Resurgam	113

P. M.

Farley	117